MW01051094

The Darkest Pastoral

JOHN KINSELLA

The Darkest Pastoral

SELECTED POEMS

 **W. W. NORTON & COMPANY**

Independent Publishers Since 1923

In memory of Marjorie Perloff

Preface © by Marjorie Perloff
Copyright © 2025 by John Kinsella

Printed in the United States of America
First Edition

Poems from *Shades of the Sublime & Beautiful* © 2008; *Armour* © 2011; *Sack* © 2014; *Drowning in Wheat: Selected Poems* © 2016; *Insomnia* © 2019. Reprinted with the permission of Picador Press (London).

The quote on page 237 from *The Argonautica* by Apollonius Rhodius is taken from the R. C. Seaton translation (1912).

For information about permission to reproduce selections from this book, write to Permissions, W. W. Norton & Company, Inc., 500 Fifth Avenue, New York, NY 10110

For information about special discounts for bulk purchases, please contact W. W. Norton Special Sales at specialsales@wwnorton.com or 800-233-4830

Manufacturing by Lake Book Manufacturing
Book design by Chris Welch
Production manager: Lauren Abbate

ISBN: 978-1-324-08929-2

W. W. Norton & Company, Inc.
500 Fifth Avenue, New York, NY 10110
www.wwnorton.com

W. W. Norton & Company Ltd.
15 Carlisle Street, London W1D 3BS

10 9 8 7 6 5 4 3 2 1

CONTENTS

FOREWORD

I have always been a little suspicious of the "new" eco-poetry. So much of it relies upon an angry, high-minded moral posture toward an anonymous "them"—those insensitive others who have no respect for the animal-vegetable-mineral kingdom, whereas the "I" who speaks *understands* the perils that beset "our planet" in the anthropocene—a term I especially dislike because it implies that only recently have human beings, led astray by the possibilities of our modern technism (Heidegger's term), set out to destroy the natural world.

John Kinsella is different. Surely the most remarkable eco-poet writing in English today, he is perhaps best understood as a great nature poet in the Wordsworthian tradition. His ability to identify with "white butterflies" and "wild radishes," with "blue-ringed octopi," "[k]angaroos in torchlight" and the "southern carpet python," is quite uncanny: not since D. H. Lawrence has any poet written so tellingly and intimately of "birds, beasts, and flowers." At the same time, Kinsella is painfully aware of "the mechanism driving / the rust of ironface, feeding the surface's scrub, / slipped buttresses, cliff faces . . . threatening the pristine catchment: / the quarry top seeking to cover the wounds" ("Catchment"). What Wordsworth called "those obstinate questionings / Of sense and outward things" are very much Kinsella's too, the difference being that the latter, writing at the turn of the twenty-first century, also dissects the machinery and the chemicals now designed to destroy the natural world and its inhabitants as expeditiously as possible.

But all is by no means gloom. Take those early poems about finches that open this collection. Here is the second one, "Finch Colony":

The *leaves*, like wire, are so tangled
we dare not venture too far into their heart

where flashes of song and dull colour
betray a whole family of finches.

We hold our breath
and become statues.

Is this fear of disturbing their peace
Or of a delicate raid from unknown spaces?

Finches are very small birds, difficult to spot under the wirelike tangle of *leaves* under which they nest: we must "hold our breath / and become statues" if we hope to become witnesses to their private world. From our perspective, care must be taken not to "disturb their peace," but from theirs, even such minimal intervention may well seem like "a delicate raid from unknown spaces." The slant rhyming of "peace"/"spaces" underscores this telling difference.

Or take the minimalist "A Rare Sight," written a few years later:

The bird seen first time here
in forty years sings lightly
on the wire, you turn to touch
the shoulder of a friend
and turning back together
find nothing but sky
and wire trembling.

The bird in question hasn't been seen in Kinsella's neighborhood for forty years, and yet one instant of distraction, and there is "nothing but sky / and wire trembling." "It is my duty," as Frank O'Hara put it, "to be attentive. I am needed by things as the sky must be above the earth."

This aesthetic of *attention* is especially striking in Kinsella's weather poems. "Fog," a poem of twelve tercets, begins:

For all its lymphatic nature
fog appears rapidly and spreads
its shroud tightly about the farm.

Lymph: the fluid in the vessels that transport from organs that contain lymphoid tissue is a pale white: just so, the fog rapidly covers the farmland in its tight white "shroud." Yet "blinding" as this "shroud" is, the fog's body itself is also felt as "unguent" (tercet 2)—like a balm that protects both sheep and people under its cover. In defining the feel of fog, Kinsella takes all five senses into account: "Wood smoke fails to coerce / its opacity and drops moistly." "Apparently sectile"—neatly cuttable into sections—the fog "flinches/ though heals instantly." To read this poem is to feel as if no one had ever really *seen* fog before!

In this mystery world, the poet is "A submariner," who "walk[s] the ocean's floor," even as "the sun, a limp beacon, drifts / to the rim of the system." The scene, tightly etched with a minimal number of nouns, adjectives, and verbs, becomes more and more surreal, the ground under the poet's feet "sink[ing]" and "thicken[ing]" even as "the fog burns my skin." And yet, despite all its seeming destructiveness, this "living entity" turns out to be a friendly presence, and the poet is able to "move steadily / on, confident that I will emerge / without a mark on my body."

Fog is a common enough Romantic topos, a familiar symbol of confusion, bewilderment, blindness, obstruction. Yet what makes this fog so remarkable is that the poem tracks its minute-by-minute evolution from the rapid formation of its "shroud" to its gradual dissipation. As readers, we participate in steady evolution and transformation: we are *there*.

A similar revisioning of a seemingly ordinary nature phenomenon occurs in "Lightning Tree":

> It's stark white in this hard
> winter light. At its base
> brackish water spreads like exposed film
> out through marshgrass & paperbarks—
> a snapped bone, it punctures the skin.

The opening lines, with their intricate assonance of long and short *i*'s, alliteration of *l*'s, and rhyming on "white"/ "light," have a riddling quality: we know from the title that Kinsella's subject is a tree hit by lightning, but its metamorphosis from living matter into *thing* is what seems so strange. Even the "brackish water" at its base "spreads like exposed film"—a piece of human-made hard celluloid. Or again the white trunk remnant recalls "snapped bone" that can "puncture the skin." On the dead tree's "splintered crown" the Great Egret "stretches, its knifed beak / piercing the cold blue sky"—

> an inverted lightning strike
> fielding its wings—
> a crucifix—hesitating,

as if held by a magnet,
then dropping into flight,
dragging lightning rod legs.

The tall Great Egret has a long S-shaped neck that indeed looks like light-ning flash, and when the long-legged bird spreads its huge wings, the shape of a crucifix is created. Ungainly on land ("as if held by a magnet"), once in flight, the Great Egret's bent, pencil-thin legs and webbed yellow feet stretch out with the look of twin lightning rods. But, in another revelatory metaphor, the "snapped bone" once a living tree, "punctures the skin." Met-onymically, the Great Egret's cruciform shape applies to the lightning tree itself, whose death is inevitable, even as the bird survives. Nature offers its own consolations for the disasters that occur.

In the 1990s, Kinsella wrote a good many poems about the animals and fish, whether goats or kangaroos, birds or snakes, of his native Western Aus-tralia. Of these my favorite is the remarkable "Sleeping with a Southern Carpet Python." This burst of memory, written in long continuous lines as if its creator cannot quite stop detailing all the particulars, recounts an inci-dent in the poet's distant past ("I am a young, embittered / father moving away from family ensconced in a low / and swampy suburb, a reclaimed rubbish tip at the base / of the Scarp"), when, as he has told us elsewhere, he was still a heavy drinker. "Driving south to stay with [his] brother," the poet "grind[s] the gravel / across the one-lane bridge," and "grow[s] steadily distracted with the brute subtleties / of dragging the back end of the car into shape." Next thing you know, although it happens "*within* / braking distance," he "skid[s] right over" an "eight-foot southern carpet python at full stretch, / slowly negotiating the road." The snake is still alive but clearly doomed to die.

Pythons are not venomous although they can bite and produce nasty infec-tions. Angry with himself but practiced in caring for all sorts of snakes, the poet lifts the python "in need of a meal, / winter shutdown fast approaching," and places it deep down in his sleeping bag. He and his brother have a long night of it, and when the drunken poet finally crawls into his sleeping bag, he is soon sleeping "deeply and in a dreamless stupor." When he wakes the next morning, "clutching / the walls of my cocoon close," his "synapses tuning / to the expectation of snake at my feet," his bag is empty! How can that be? "I reach for my glasses and focus" and lo and behold:

The southern
carpet python, carpet snake of my childhood

I saw often on the farm coiled around log rafters
in the hay barn, rat-hunter and friend of the farmer,
warder-off of ill charms of presence, is sliding
alongside the walls, rounding the square room,
full of my body-warmth and raring to go.

As someone unfamiliar with snakes, I found this final twist terrifying.
What? The supposedly all but dead snake, stored in the sleeping bag under-
neath the "poikilothermic" narrator, is not only alive but "sliding / along-
side the walls" and "raring to go"? How could the poet have made it through
the night? And now what?

It is a frightening, but also a very funny, moment. The reader senses
that, however creepy the image of the python crawling the walls, the poet
will cope, will take care of the snake. Indeed, he is happy to see it alive, his
tolerance for reptiles, birds, and insects being enormous. It is, rather, the
object world that arouses his contempt. "The Bulldozer Poem"—a poem
now famous for its brilliant satire of the machine world that engulfs us—
makes its case by treating those ugly vehicles as human beings so as to
underscore their cruelty. Bulldozers "rend flesh," they "grimace when they
/ tear the earth's skin," they "slice & dice," they are "vigorous / percus-
sionists, sounding the snap and boom of hollows / caving in." Bulldozers
"are compelled to do / as they are told"—how true!— "they recognise final
causes, and embrace / outcomes that put them out of work."

After seven tercets that ironically catalog these qualities, Kinsella makes
a turn and addresses the bulldozer directly in a mock Pindaric ode:

O *continuous tracked tractor,*

O *S* and *U* blades, each to his orders, his skillset. Communal
as D9 Dozers (whose buckets uplift to asteroids waiting
to be quarried). O bulldozer! Your history! . . .

O your Makers—Cummings and Caterpillar—O great *Cat*
. . .
We must know your worldliness—working with companies
to make a world of endless horizons. It's a team effort, excoriating
an eco-system. Not even you can tackle an old-growth tall tree alone.

But we know your power, your pedigree, your sheer bloody
mindedness.

All of this is as accurate as it is funny and terrifying at once. Bulldozers are by definition *bloody-minded*, cutting up and dismembering everything in their path. They, not lions and tigers, reptiles or rats, are the monsters of our time.

I happened to be reading this astonishing poem just on the day my new neighbors, having gotten permission to tear down the lovely old house next door, announced that 3,054 cubic yards of earth were soon to be removed and hauled away from this green and wooded site, making room for the bulldozers that would remove the old foundation and level the site. A hellish notion, bloody-minded indeed, but it happens in my neighborhood every day and no one seems to bat an eyelash. Perhaps I shall have to enlist John Kinsella's help: maybe he can come to Los Angeles and stand in the path of dump truck and bulldozer, reciting his poem, even as he evidently did against the Roe 8 Highway in Western Australia.

The Darkest Pastoral closes with an exemplar from Kinsella's poem-photoessay cycles known as *Graphologies Lambent* that, along with such *calligrammes* as "Bushfire Sun," have challenged the poet for the past few decades. "I am interested," Kinsella has remarked, "in low-tech engagements with degrees of light. . . . Not just through seeing, but experiencing exposure." In *Graphologies Lambent* the photo-poem "The extravagant rectitude of bees," with its four images—three black-and-white and the second one in color—is accompanied by the following note:

> That same persistent nest of European honeybees in a very old York gum at Jam Tree Gully where we live on Ballardong Noongar land (near Whadjuk and Yued countries) is one I accidentally stirred in passing when we first arrived, and I ended up being stung multiple times because of this surprise encounter. I know the nest is there now, as it has been for so long, and I am always careful around it —a matter of respect as much as anything else. Bees don't survive stinging. I won't be responsible for any bee death. As a consequence of that first encounter, I have altered my path and my manner of movement. I see outside my usual colour range. I have tried to shift the spectrum.

The poem, written in open couplets, begins by recounting this first encounter when Kinsella was stung by the bees "in the hollow of a middle-aged York gum." The photographs—especially the second one, "azure of the sky and chlorophyll of canopy / reddened in the cramped darkness"—are disturbing, for however respectfully Kinsella writes of the bees in the note above, their image—small striped yellow-brown-blue pellets, crawling around the edges of the nasty dark hole in the ugly gnarled tree trunk—is, at least to my mind, repulsive. Far from illustrating the text, these images belong to nightmare.

But Kinsella evidently sees it differently, for he concludes:

These patterns I word into fields,
smears lost in thumbprints;

autonomous as collectives,
glorious in memory of tree.

This portrait of descent,
realigning of exits.

However we interpret this "realigning of exits," with its echo of "descent," surely we can agree that the graphology in question is unforgettable: an image from Lethe, as Ezra Pound would call it, whose sting has not gone away. These are great ecological poems, whose wide sweep becomes increasingly astonishing as the years go by. At this writing, John Kinsella is a mere sixty. Who knows what is yet to come?

Marjorie Perloff

The Darkest Pastoral

Finches

Down below the dam
there is nothing but salt,
a slow encroachment.

Fighting back, my cousins
have surrounded it
with a ring of trees.

At its centre
lives a colony of finches,
buried in tamarisks.

FINCH COLONY

The *leaves*, like wire, are so tangled
we dare not venture too far into their heart
where flashes of song and dull colour
betray a whole family of finches.

We hold our breath
and become statues.

Is this fear of disturbing their peace
or of a delicate raid from unknown spaces?

FINCH FLIGHT

To join the finch
in his tenuous kingdom
amongst tamarisks,
the hot snow of salt

You must gather
trajectory and direction,
sharp summer flights

Exile yourself
from the wind's hand.

FINCH DEATH

The dead finch lies on salt,
tight winged and stretched.

The others shimmer
loosely in heat

the salt's white mystery
coveting tin cans, skull of sheep.

Slowly, death rides this hot glacier
further and further away.

Night Parrots

If at all, then fringe dwellers
   of the centre.
Ghosts of samphire, navigators
of the star-clustered tussocks.
Of salty marsh, limestone niches,
   and acrid airs.

If at all, then flitting obscurely
the rims of water tanks, the outlands
of spotlights and filaments of powerlines . . .
in brief nocturnal flight, with *long
drawn out mournful whistle.*

If at all, then moths in a paper lantern.

Inland

Inland: storm tides,
ghosts of a sheep weather
alert, the roads uncertain

families cutting the outback
gravel on Sunday mornings,
the old man plying the same track
to and from the session
those afternoons, evenings
(McHenry skidded into a thickset
mallee after a few too many
and was forced to sell up)

On the cusp of summer
an uncertain breeze
rises in grey wisps
over the stubble—
the days are ashen,
moods susceptible,
though it does not take
long to get back
into the swing of things

We take the only highroad
for miles as the centre
of the primum mobile—it's
the eye of the needle
through which our lives'
itineraries must be drawn,
a kind of stone theodolite
measuring our depths beyond
the straight and narrow,
it's a place of borrowed dreams
where the marks of the spirit
have been occluded by dust—
the restless topsoil

The Myth of the Grave

I

A pair of painted quails
scurries across the quills of stubble
a flurry of rapid
eye movement

they shadow my walk
ostentatiously
lifting and dropping
into invisible alleyways

reaching the grave
I turn to catch them
curving back, stopped
by the windrows

the grave is a magnet
that switches polarity
when you reach it.

II

The epitaph is measured
by the size of the plaque,
or is it the plaque that's
measured by the epitaph?

It seems to matter.
Death becomes a question
of economy—the lavish are big
on ceremony, slight on prayer.

III

At a distance
sheep leave salt-licks
beside a dam and zigzag
down towards the shade.

Grey gums bend with the tide
of the breeze, the midday sun
would carry their doubles
to the grave and fill the urns.

The ground dries and crumbles,
a lizard darts out of a crack
and races across the paddock.
Do ashes rest easily here?

IV

A fresh grave that holds three
generations is something you question
on a first encounter. How in life
would they have felt about sharing

a single room in a shoebox flat?
Maybe, at an instant, only one soul
is resident, the others entering the bodies
of quails, exploring the wastes of stubble.

Pillars of Salt

We always look back,
attracted by that feeling
of having been there before—the roads
sinking, the soil weeping (scab on scab
lifted), fences sunk to gullies
catching the garbage of paddocks,
strainers blocked by stubble
and machinery and the rungs
of collapsed rainwater tanks / and maybe
the chimney and fireplace
of a corroded farmhouse, once
the guts of the storm, now
a salty trinket.

The salt is a frozen waste
in a place too hot for its own good,
it is the burnt-out core of earth's eye,
the excess of white blood cells.
The ball-and-chain rides lushly
over its polishing surface, even dead wood
whittles itself out of the picture.

Salt crunches like sugar-glass, the sheets
lifting on the soles of shoes (thongs scatter
pieces beyond the hope of repair)—finches
and flies quibble on the thick fingers
of salt bushes, a dugite spits
blood into the brine.

An airforce trainer jet appears,
the mantis pilot—dark eyed and wire
jawed—sets sight on the white wastes
for a strafing run: diving, pulling out
abruptly, refusing to consummate.

                              Salt
explodes silently, with the animation

of an inorganic life, a sheep's skull no more
than its signature, refugees already
climbing towards the sun
on pillars of salt.

Catchment

I ZONE

In a catchment zone the keepers
must keep clean houses, sweeping
soot from the roots, scouring
granite outcrops regularly.

The catchment's focus—a saline pool,
comfortable in its illusion of deep, clear water—
sheds itself in the stubs of severed trees
hedging the waterline.

II QUARRY

Examining the dross of a quarry
(the coarse and fine sizes), we may grasp
what it is that has reduced things to this:

the panorama sliced away in cross section,
exposing the roots in their bed of rock;
or in the deeper layers, the mechanism driving
the rust of ironface, feeding the surface's scrub,
slipped buttresses, cliff faces . . .
                       the risk of overextension
threatening the pristine catchment:
the quarry top seeking to cover the wounds.

III PIPES AND VALVES

We scale the wall, rising up over the filaments
of pumping station—pipes, straitjacketed,
annelids splitting and regenerating in and out
of the slinking earth, skirting the valley,
entwining undergrowth

                              the valves feeding
from their concrete outriggers (weir-houses
inhabited by pressure gauges, clacks, and screws),
their task reason enough for existence, thoughts
on source and destination not one of their strong points.

IV THE WIDER WATERS

Sloughs of mosquitoes squeezing in and out
of sluices in a hillside cast barely
a collective shadow over the catchment.

At the foot of a spillway, past seasons
wallow in brackish puddles, raft insects
eke out sketchy existences
                              thin lines of pines
cling to retainer walls.

From the summit—the barrier neither moulded nor bound
by roots, but soldered to the squared shoulders
of valley—we look to the liquid centre: wind slicks
flattening the ripples, ironing them out, wiping
the corrugated glass clean, darning patches
on the wider waters.

A Field of White Butterflies

There is a lot of mystery in me . . .
he explains, peering deep into my eyes.
As a child I would examine the smallest
things, things that would not ordinarily
be seen. My mother would tell the neighbours
that I was a daydreamer, there was no other way
of explaining it. That was in a very
cold place, high in the mountains
above Dalmatia in Yugoslavia.
I came here when I was eighteen
looking for work. I knew about
the languages of animals and plants.

Three seasons ago you couldn't
look at this paddock without seeing
a white butterfly—consuming, crowding
even themselves out of existence.
Last season I saw two, two white butterflies
in the whole year. This year the Monarch
will come, mark my words—wandering
down over the hills, settling
pince-nez on the potato flowers.
You see, where people settle
imbalance follows, the air
being full of white butterflies,
or there being no white butterflies at all.

Ibis

An ibis picks between thin veins
of grass surfacing on open ground,
recently upturned, nourished in mist
and exhumed by the morning sun.

Stilt-legged it stalks on a pivot,
graceful in its geometrics.
It is difficult to pinpoint
the centre of balance,
which imparts a life of its own.

In flight it lunges slowly
as though it were not meant
to be airborne, its legs
tight outriggers, mouthpiece
a curved pipette
drawing and discharging
the grey-blue sky.

I also remain afloat
—an ibis—riding the crests
and troughs of a changing surface,
settling on aspects of thought,
treading lightly the outskirts.

Plumburst

The neat greens of Monument Hill
roll into sea, over the rise the soft rain
of plumfall deceives us in its groundburst.

If lightning strikes from the ground up,
and Heaven is but an irritation that prompts
its angry spark, then plums are born
dishevelled on the ground and rise
towards perfection . . .

Out of the range of rising plums
we mark the territory of the garden,
testing caprock with Judas trees,
pacing out melon runs. Behind us a block
of flats hums into dusk and the sun
bursts a plum mid-flight.

Of

Of emulsifiers and preservatives
extracted from boiled-down animal,
of houses with walls of horse hair
and thongs of leather to restrain
the tortured awning,
of feet covered in dead cow,
kangaroo, crocodile . . .
the business of pig-skin briefcases,
of those whose guilt lay in fish,
of those sucking the nectars
of sacred beasts,
of the differences between *clean* and *dirty* flesh,
of those who seek truth in the burnt offering,
of 'perfect and upright' Job, slaughterer
who sought to appease over and over,
of *Julius Civilus with a Dead Cock*
arrogantly accepting what *is*
over and over, back and forth, to and fro.

Window Shopping at the Taxidermist's

The permeable glass—sieve-like—drains
the liquid light, a fluid more precious
than formaldehyde, the smell of life . . .
A grimace or a grin stretches like a trap,
and as a backdrop a deer dispenses
with its claim to needing a heart,
it's only there from the neck up,
though its eyes are sharp, senses finely
tuned, nervousness held in check
through a familiarity born of sharing
a display case with a pack of wolves.
The window shoppers hunt amongst the grime
of the city's unglamorous side, their prey
the glimmering skin, the combed and shining—
here they show their skill, knowing
where to bag the finest trophy.

Warhol at Wheatlands

He's polite looking over the Polaroids
saying gee & fantastic, though always
standing close to the warm glow

of the WonderHeat as the flames
lick the self-cleansing glass.
It's winter down here & the sudden

change has left him wanting. Fog
creeps up from the gullies & toupées
the thinly pastured soil. It doesn't

remind him of America at all. But there's
a show on television about New York so
we stare silently, maybe he's asleep

behind his dark glasses? Wish Tom
& Nicole were here. He likes the laser
prints of Venice cluttering the hallway,

the sun a luminous patch trying
to break through the dank cotton air
& the security film on the windows.

Deadlocks & hardened glass make him feel
comfortable, though being locked inside
with Winchester rifles has him tinfoiling

his bedroom—he asks one of us but we're
getting ready for seeding & can't spare a moment.
Ringnecked parrots sit in the fruit trees

& he asks if *they're* famous. But he
doesn't talk much (really). Asked about Marilyn
he shuffles uncomfortably—outside, in the

spaces between parrots & fruit trees
the stubble rots & the day fails
   to sparkle.

Sexual Politics in Eadweard Muybridge's *Man Walking, After Traumatism of the Head*

1

He could easily be
A man walking, after traumatism
Of the head.
There's something vaguely Platonic about this.
Francis Bacon, lip-synching
His way through smugness, injecting passion and/or lust
Into Muybridge's studies of wrestlers: 'Actually,
Michelangelo and Muybridge
Are mixed up in my
Mind together, and so I perhaps
Could learn about positions
From Muybridge
And learn about the ampleness,
The grandeur of form
From Michelangelo . . .' This is not tongue-in-cheek,
And why should it be? she cries.
At the end of the day
Folly counts for nothing, she says
Majestically, the banana light glowing
Sedately by the bedhead, Foucault
Powerless and fading.

2

What moral autonomy remains
As, from frame to frame,
He walks. Why aren't you a panel beater?
She asks as your last thought spills
To the floor and scatters.

Muybridge considered
Leland Stanford's Quest To Prove

All Four Legs Of A Trotting Horse
Are Off The Ground Simultaneously
At A Particular Moment . . . earlier
He'd been a fly on the wall
As Muybridge blew his wife's
Dashing, cavalier lover away . . .
'omne animal triste post coitum'.

Sadness comes quickly
And he wonders about
The contents of his blood.
And panel beaters would find
The passive role
Difficult
To shape.

3

Sharing a cell with lust
In the prison of desire
He remarked that the form
Of his cell-mate was a little peculiar:
Casanova moving with the gait
Of one who has succumbed
To animal locomotion, an electro-photographic
Investigation of consecutive phases
Of animal movement.

She says that he measures progress
With his penis, a well-oiled dip stick:
Her body absorbing the entire jungle
Of his body which is ecologically sound,
Creeping out of its rich enclave
And seeking to make the barren lush.
He believes that you can't get off

On rape, that violence is mental
Sickness.
I like his manners—c'est tout—
She confesses.

4

A skull fractured
Does not necessarily
Mean liberation
On the afterdeath plane
Nor freedom for the oppressed mind.
LSD, a *freak* in disguise,
Denies the mind is lodged
In the skull, that it is
Part of the body. The dozen or so
Blotters found in his pocket
Have nothing to do
With his portfolio
Of deviance.
He's on top of it,
And knows the yellow haze
Suppressing the landscape
Is merely ash
In the upper-atmosphere.
The signature is this: it hurts
To cum on bad acid, but did that
Ever deter you?

5

His head is traumatised
By dehydration, his brain shrinking.
Starvation has frayed the linkages

Between spinal cortex and legs.
His walk is one of decline
Interrupted by hope.
He feels spent and thin.
Men eat to vomit and vomit to eat,
Seneca tells us; and no woman can be too rich or too thin.
Chastity is starvation
Starvation is traumatism of the head.

6

She hates the hype
But loves the splendour:
The page written she relinquishes
Her rights to the material
Inherently hers. The moral community
Is concerned only with growth
At the end of the day—he tells them
That he is hers and couldn't give a shit.
Does she reciprocate? they say.
Would you—a man walking,
With a traumatism of the head?

7

Underwire bras and jockstraps
Entangle a chicken desperately
Lunging, a torpedo already
Within range of its tail feathers,
Rudely muzzling its way
Through a sea of discharge.
So, this is love? it asks.
Muybridge screams from his observation post
'Keep the bloody thing within the gridwork!

Calibrate, calibrate! for God's sake
It's all comparative.' Stripping off
He rushes the chicken and wrestles it,
'Damn the torpedoes, keep the cameras rolling!'
Duchamp's Nude descends a staircase
While Meissonier, de Neuville, Detaille,
Remington, Malevich, and Giacomo Balla,
Watch on excitedly.

8

When size doesn't matter
You'd better start asking questions.
I mean, it's all or nothing
Isn't it. As for what's behind it . . .
A magnet does have two poles.
Self-control, the object of pleasure:
Every orgasm a spot in time
Without the lacework.
And this all about walking,
With a traumatism of the head,
The lexicon spread as three rednecks
Smash you over the skull with iron-knuckled
Fists, or an overdose of speed threatens
To burst capillaries, or glass lodged in a crescent
Below your left eye dislodges and unplugs
The contents of your identity.
The time lapse between frames shortens
And your collapse is traced
More minutely. Hasten slowly.

9

Porn is the Theory.
Rape is the Practice.
A sign held by a youth
In Minneapolis.
A skirt stained with sweat
Radiates in a bath
Of yellow dye.
The gate is locked,
The fences high.
She, sunbaking,
Looks over her shoulder,
Her tan slipping away:
In a tree perches
Her neighbour,
A glint in his eye.

10

Stripping thought
He dreamt an anthology,
Visual and responsive.
Reflections on the obvious.
A spring day and I'm full of hate.
Stuff like that.
He would include
A photograph by Muybridge,
(Who after disposing of Major Larkyns
Apologised to the ladies
And settled to a newspaper).
Though not one of his locomotion
Sequences, whose implication
Goes beyond a book, but of the *Colorado*
In dry dock accompanied by an anonymous

Muybridge on Contemplation Rock
Later used as proof of madness.
And on the title page a quote
From the *San Francisco Daily*
Evening Post: 'Little
Did Muybridge dream
As he bent over
The bedside of his wife
And he caressed her,
That Larkyns' kisses
Were yet fresh and hot
Upon her lips'.

Lavender Mist

after Jackson Pollock

An overcast day scripted by night.
Drizzle drifts in over the coast,
       jacketing factories,
       apartments & barns
with propylene. Lavender mist,
so sickly sweet, read in a trance, fault-
       lines threatening to burst,
       shell-craters unravelling.
What forces moving across borders?
Lavender mist is the movement before death,
       shrapnel silently
       cutting its way
through lace curtains while you look
down onto a radioactive sea—lavender mist,
       potpourri,
       swallowing
the wharves, the first waves of the cold war
& their lurid afterglow.

On Andy Warhol's *Marilyn Six-Pack*

Rip top lips—the movement is piracy.
An early cut—an addict's selective

disclosure. A perfect pose concealing
popular truths, the value of trashy

synthetic polymer makeup, canvas
skin and silkscreened hair. A six-pack's hazy

suppression of class and style, like seeing
the world in black and white. Quick! Look at me!

it pleads with a fizzing hiss. If you stand
long enough success will expose itself.

The pout shapes the plates, but the eyelids take
the weight—suspended languidly below

the constructed eyebrows. O Marilyn—
six tabs without the blister packaging.

Chillies

1. THE CONSERVATIVE

Not supplicants but receptors—
wanton idols
raising red tribute, the crossover
green-orange, a query
in need of editing, ingesting the anger
and soil's biteback, the soil
drinking a market economy
red being more marketable
(a humorous colour), a conservative
hotbed wanting to cling
but conscious of the constituents'
response, hasten slowly.

2. THE MIDDLE GROUND

Or chillies without seeds.
Rarely as hot, colour
as of chrysoprase, deeply attractive,
mimicking the wrought heart
of compassion.
You don't need a glass of water
even if you'd
like to think so.

3. THE RADICAL

Green is the heat,
each chilli a piece,
sweat and a repeating stomach
something to flaunt.
You grow your own
but despite rumours

don't plant on the full moon.
Slim canisters
of motivation, slick grenades
imploding.

RESIDUE

I am addicted
to chillies.
I break a red chilli
with my fingers
and spread it
through my meal.
Another false god
under the pine trees.

A friend needles me
another can barely
contain her laughter.
I wipe my eyes, a seed
lodges in a tear duct.
My tears are red
and pungent.
The seeds
are the hottest
part.

THE LIBERATING CHILLIES

She hates them.
I'm addicted
grow my own
and am fascinated
by the way green turns

almost black before
the sun liberates
the red. My love
of the word "wicked"
evolves from chillies.
A bad experience
with bird's eyes
actually. Ah, little
bull's horn rhytons,
quivers of fertility
permanently erect—the fruit
mocking the delicate flower.
But I burn
my self—the seeds
hold the sharpest power
and you must sacrifice
aesthetics for pleasure.
I burn from the inside out.

CHILLI HUNT

She says that chillies
are a form of madness—
that like a crazed dog I froth
at the thought of them.
A bizarre addiction.

Maybe. Last night the moon
full if slightly kinked,
marked a kris on the skins
of chillies bent towards
its grasp, fine metal reaching

for the loadstone. Ah that crazy
tattooist the moon. Chillies

are neither mad nor sane
if they show reverence for its
persistence. For today

I hunt without words. I feel
her watching over my shoulder,
skirts teasing the grass,
the skin on my back
erupting. I continue breaking

the stalks, collecting. Some
for immediate use, others for
drying. I know the full-blown
moon hunts in the back of her
eyes, that chillies a deeper red
than mine mark time and call her
to leave me to a minor harvest.

CHILLI CATHARSIS

It fortifies my blood
against the heat
of separation—
a placebo.
Fire against fire.
Unleash your dark
lightning: anti-sex,
space condensed ultra
or even collapsed.
I take I take.
This the poet
abusing language
for the sake of stasis—
the symbol as solid
as you wish. The devil's tool,
the devil's number.

Concrete. The sculptured
chilli. Like falling
on your own sword.
The heat the heat.
Fall into my burnt body
and torch your anger,
a chilli dance
for our son—fantasia
purified. Clean
but cold. Our sweat ice
on swollen cheeks. Chillies
charred at our feet.

HEREDITARY CHILLIES/PREDESTINATION

That in their infancy
the plants are so vulnerable
appeals to me—the leaf-eaters
and sap-suckers of the garden
will defoliate, destalk,
and wizen before the sun
has risen. But fruiting,
they are rarely bothered.
But this of course is not
so remarkable when considered
comparatively. Vulnerability
heightens savagery—the cute
lion cub et al. The other
thing that fascinates me
is their sense of fait accompli—
but there is nothing in my
family tree to suggest
an onslaught of chilli.
Neither my mother nor father
can stomach them.

ARCHETYPAL CHILLIES

Are etched deep within
the human psyche—burning
seedcases bursting and re-locating
their ornamental hue. I open my
skull to your inquisitive gaze—
look, here are my chillies,
red and foreboding, hungry
for the light. See, you've done
me a favour—chillies breed on lies
but thrive on truth. They like it
both ways. Ah, if only
you'd admit to chillies—then,
then you'd understand me. The rhetoric
would flower superbly and I'd sing.
Christ, I'd sing. And you'd hear me
no matter where you hid. Your dreams
would be coloured by my song. Of chillies
and their involvement with the growth
of our souls. Of chillies and their
need for nurturing. Of the bitterness
they harvest from rejection. For this
is their strength—they are of you and I,
they are the sun's subtle rays
grown both cold and hot, they
like it both ways.

TRANSCENDENTAL CHILLIES

The weather's changing
so chillies redden
slowly. I do not expect
them to ripen according
to my programme—though I'm
told this is my way.
But a few warm days
and you can be almost
guaranteed to find them
moving from state to state.
A green chilli flatlining
and finding the other side
tolerable. Easter Friday.
The heavy clouds are rolling in.
They predicted that a week ago.
Here, try a chilli—they're
deadly at this time of year—
the pride of the garden—corn
long since finished, the last rays
of summer spilling from over-ripe
tomatoes, lettuces shaking their
seedy arms, their heads embalmed
about thickened stalks
while chillies—majestic—daggers
awaiting the sunlight, hone
their skills in the weakening light.

THE POLICE BUSTED ME WITH A CHILLI IN MY POCKET

It'd been through the wash—it was
in fact half-a-chilli
looking fibrous and not a little
washed out. But there was
no doubting it was a chilli,
I accepted that—no need
for laboratory tests, the eye
and honesty adequate analysis.
So, why do you do it?
they asked. I dunno, just a habit
I guess. The sun dropped below
the horizon like a billiard ball.
The chilli glowed in a hand.
One of them rubbed his eyes and they
began to sting. We'll have you for assault
they said.

The Ascension of Sheep

The sun has dragged
the fog away
and now the sheep
in sodden clothes may

fleece the farmer—
who warm by the fire
tallies heads and prices
and thinks about slaughter—

each soul taken upwards
from its fertile
body—columns of mist
like pillars of a temple.

Come midday they'll
have dried right through
and follow the trail
down to the dam

where the water
refills the empty chamber
where the soul
could never feel secure.

Hoppers and Gargoyles

A screw drives the lupins towards the chute,
lupins spill into the hopper, an auger drags
them upwards towards the spout, lupins spill
into the silo. These are the facts, or facts
as they seem to the farmer who follows
the tried-and-true procedure, believes
what his eyes tell him, and is satisfied
with the end result. These are the facts
as his father has told him, neighbours confirm.

Another view, another set of facts: the gargoyle
masquerading as a spout draws all into its mouth
and spits it back, the hopper—its belly—endlessly
fuelled by the reaper who, disguised as a farmer,
cannot be content with endless death, but rather
gains its pleasure from the neighbours who believe
what they tell the farmer, who stare at the spout
and see no more than lupins filling his coffers.

Rock Picking: Building Cairns

The spine is best kept straight—
the weight of granite will damage
vertebrae, stretch the spinal cord.
    Let the knees do the work,
legs levering the load from ground
to trailer dragged at a crawl behind
    the Massey Ferguson tractor.

Cairnwards we move over the paddock,
building these self-contained environments
for snakes, spiders, and bush-wise architects.
    Ground lost is ground gained,
these cairns are completely functional.
Satellite cities linked by machinery that's
    commuter friendly if unpredictable.

Rune stones carefully placed, oblatory,
offerings for local deaths—accidents at harvest,
on gravel roads, wild tractor's overturning,
augers catching a hand and swallowing flesh.
    And deities only farmers know.

Dried lichen and sweat mix to cement a cairn.
The surface suppressing the glitter of quartz—
pink, rose, white, transparent. Sources of warmth
these repositories of micro-chip technology
(unharnessed) attract infrared telescopics,
blood coursing through their Frankenstein

monster bodies, distracting the predator's weapon
as it roams in search of foxes and rabbits.
Cairns—where youths empty swollen bladders
drunkenly into the fissures and cast amber bottles
into cobwebbed abysses, where wild oats grow at
impossible angles and lure the sun into darkness.

As I rock pick I unravel these pictures and spread
them to all corners of the paddock. I coin phrases,
devise anecdotes, invest the ups and downs of my
life in these cairns constructed from the landscape's
    wreckage, place sheep skulls on summits.

Alone, I feed these rowdy cities the stuff
of my blisters, sign the structures with broken
fingers, convert plans to ash and scatter
    them about the foundations.
Softly softly I sing the ruins of our
pampered anatomies, draw strength from the
    harsh realities of empire building.

And following duskfall, the tractor
and trailer no longer visible, I climb
onto the motorbike and drape myself over
    the seat—a bag of bones
slung over the tray of an iron jinker.
As the tractor comes into focus the cairns
    retreat—pyramids of the outback.

A Rare Sight

The bird seen first time here
in forty years sings lightly
on the wire, you turn to touch
the shoulder of a friend
and turning back together
find nothing but sky
and wire trembling.

The Silo

Visitors, as if they knew, never remarked
on the old silo with its rammed earth walls
and high thatched roof, incongruous amongst
the new machinery and silver field bins.
Nor the workers brought in at harvest time,
trucks rolling past the ghostly whimperings,
snarls and sharp howls cutting the thick silo's
baffling. Nor when a bumper harvest filled
every bin and the farmer was hungry
for space—no one ever mentioned bringing
the old silo back into service. This
had been the way for as far back as could
be remembered. Thin sprays of baby's breath
grew around its foundations, while wedding
bouquet sprouted bizarrely from the grey
mat of thatching. The sun had bleached the walls
bone-white while the path to the heavily
bolted door was of red earth, a long thin
stream of unhealthy blood. Before those storms
which brew thickly on summer evenings
red-tailed black cockatoos settled in waves,
sparking the straw like a volcano, dark
fire erupting from the heart of the white
silo, trembling with energy deeper
than any anchorage earth could offer.
And lightning dragging a moon's bleak halo
to dampen the eruption, with thunder
echoing out over the bare paddocks
towards the farmhouse where an old farmer
consoled his bitter wife on the fly-proof
verandah, cursing the cockatoos, hands
describing a prison from which neither
could hope for parole, petition, release.

Why They Stripped the Last Trees
from the Banks of the Creek

They stripped the last trees
from the banks of this creek
twenty years ago. The old man
couldn't stand the thought
of bare paddocks with a creek
covered by trees slap bang
in the middle of them.
A kind of guilt I guess.
Anyway, he was old
and we humoured him—
chains, rabbit rippers,
chainsaws. We cleared
those banks until the water
ran a stale sort of red.
Until salt crept into
the surrounding soaks.
Furious he was—the salt
left lines on the bath,
the soap wouldn't lather.

Fog

For all its lymphatic nature
fog appears rapidly and spreads
its shroud tightly about the farm.

And though blinding, sheep and people
stumble smoothly through its unguent
body. Wood smoke fails to coerce

its opacity and drops moistly.
Apparently sectile it flinches
though heals instantly.

You drink its flesh with every breath.
Settling on low ground it climbs
to the peaks of hills and spills,

using trees and granite outcrops
as hungry boards. A submariner,
I walk the ocean's floor.

The fog thickens about the family
graves, tarnishing plaques
and chilling icons to the bone.

Finches zip like apparitions,
the sun, a limp beacon, drifts
to the rim of the system.

I mark the blurred silver
of a galvanised tank
as a point for navigation

and set off through the red flesh
of failing saltbush, over a carpet
of mustard she-oak needles.

The ground sinks and thickens.
In this quasi-world I hesitate—
as the fog burns my skin I sense

a fire's shadow and hear water
crackling as it fuels the mass
of liquid flame. A living entity

the fog accepts me—I move steadily
on, confident that I will emerge
without a mark on my body.

Alf Reckons Lucy's the Bloke

Alf reckons Lucy's the bloke.
'She's the one with the balls,'
he says spitting into the cattle
grid.
      'Yeh, I reckon Lucy's the bloke.
That Anna's like my missus—always
complaining but big-hearted and goddamn
nice to the children. Stays at home.
That Lucy—Christ, she ploughs
and seeds and waters the stock.
She handles a header as well
as Geoff, myself, or Jock.
You've got to hand it to her.
Yeh, I reckon Lucy's the bloke.'

Goading Storms out of a Darkening Field

Goading storms out of a darkening field,
Cockeyed bobs seeding the salt, the farmer
Cursing the dry, cursing the bitter yield.

And while lightning would savage him with skilled
Thrusts, and floods strip the topsoil, it's better
Goading storms out of a darkening field

Than sit distraught on the verandah, killed
By the 'quitter's syndrome'—it's much safer
Cursing the dry, cursing the bitter yield.

Field bins empty, coffers bare, should have sold
Two years back when prices were halfway there.
Goading storms out of a darkening field.

Red harvest, charred hills, dry wells filled and sealed.
Sheep on their last legs. Dams crusted over.
Cursing the dry, cursing the bitter yield.

It's tempting when prayers and patience have failed,
Diviners have lost track of ground water.
Goading storms out of a darkening field.
Cursing the dry, cursing the bitter yield.

Parrot Deaths

1.

Parrot deaths aren't mentioned
on this stretch of road, especially
in summer when vast scoured

fields leave only trees on the gravel,
long thin shadows that sprout rosellas
and 'twenty-eights' in families,

when foliage is the emerald green
of chests exploding their small fists
against the windows of the car.

2.

Or cracked under the wheel
spread-eagled, the sharp skull crack,
auguring spilt grain

from gravel or brief stretches
of asphalt, harvesting the write-offs,
the contractors thumping their trucks

over potholes and corrugations
on their way to the silos. Either gold,
orange, or blood-red sunsets erase death.

3.

U-turn or reverse, scrape the red breast
of a rosella into the palm of your hand.
From here it's only a matter of moments

before breath suspends its downward slide,
brief glance of startled wonder,
head lapsing into the swings

of a slow pendulum. Its wise-cracking beak
a husk for the salted kernel of its tongue,
still too tight to let death loose.

Skeleton weed/generative grammar

I FINITE-STATE

The 'i' takes in what is said—
yes, it is easily led
across the floors of discourse
only to find itself a force
easily reckoned with: there's
no point in stock-taking arrears
as fleshly interests tell you
nothing except acceptability & taboo.
Take skeleton weed infesting
the crop—rosette of basal
leaves unleashing a fatal
stem with *daisy-like* flowers
that drop (into) parachute clusters
of seeds. One missed when
they scour the field (men
& women anonymously-clothed
seated on a spidery raft dragged
behind a plodding tractor,
monotony testing the free-will factor),
can lead to disaster.

II PHRASE-STRUCTURE

{[((analyz)ing)] [the ((constituent)s)]}
we examine(?) the wool of sheep
for free-loading skeleton-weed seeds,
their teeth specifically designed
for wool: the ag department
have decided they ARE selective
though admit our investigations
will help their 'research'.

III TRANSFORMATIONAL

One year the farmer asked us if we
felt guilty for missing one & hence ruining
his would-have-been bumper crop.
Quarantined the following year. Losing
his unseeded would-be bumper crop.
Ruining his credit rating. His marriage.
His son's & daughter's places
at their exclusive city boarding
schools. His problem with alcohol.
His subsequent breakdown
& hospitalization. (?) We remained
& still remain passive. Still we remained
& remain passive. But we [look(ed)] deeply,
collectively & independently
into our SELVES. Our silence
was an utterance of a loud inner speech.
A loud inner speech was an utterance
of our silence. Speaking for myself,
I've included in my lexicon of guilt
the following: what I feel today
will I feel tomorrow? And those tight
yellow flowers: so beautiful on the wiry
structures they call 'skeleton weed.'

A Zone Essay on Prohibition and Purity

Scrutiny discouraged or forbidden, the polluted privilege
flowing dissolute across: hard water that sticks and breaks
down only silent dirt, the anxious metaphors, access
as privilege in the Landsat designated open spaces,
closed in small but concentrated openings, as poets
labour in innocence in wrath, trans the substance
of drink and counter meals in pubs on the main highway,
up the banner to catch the eye of the tv camera,
we drink our fences though some buy filters or drums
of mineral water at service stations, despite our privilege
reason qualifies stability as deeper deeper into the dope-infested
dark dank forest they go, towards the ochre banks
and flat blue tableaux, zoning in emergent chemicals
like rancid paraphernalia in the political act: take
the prophetic gravel landscape as only rangers do
as monks in Meteora or at Qumrān or the caves
of Saint Anthony testing theories of abjection & temptation
without resonance, not a sound to be had spreading
colloquially out in the rising flood of scape, of tableau,
of dehydration in the place where water cannot be drunk
for purity's sake. Here the I redefines its place
and splits itself as process, the rapid oxidation, the gas
as haze just above the delinquent surfaces, the signed
public spaces, focussing as nationhood the mutual place
like boastful decadence, hysterical in the priming
of labels against Gabriele d'Annunzio plagiarizing
the sacred texts, against the artistry of a degenerate
world lying in wait, redgum sap levered from the massive
trunk with a long knife in South Dandalup, nearby
the narrowing spillway and blue mechanics of the flood-
gates, control-column fluted and space-aged
and off limits, ruminating over the window of the dam,
'the fascist glorification of the inhuman' quoting
against the likely source, as the streams still slip
from seams in rock, the under-divined runnels
beneath the deforming forest floor, spores of bracken fern
falling like quotes in the need for pure appropriations,

the common body of water placing itself at zero
in the tremor filled anti-resilience of blasted air,
birds erupting East as the front moves nearer
and refugees move into prohibited zones: as one MAN
hits the blaster [principium individuationis] against
Hazchem and 1080 foxbait and the repetition of signs
Warning Conveyor   Bauxite Mining   Blast Area
                    PROHIBITED ZONE
as understated rust-red foliage placates the crowns
of republican trees in a dying forest. Purity as intent.
They drink clean water. Company planes and pilots
tracking souls on long-lease tracks, per tonne
the complete freedom of association in the company
newsletter. Mythos as letterhead the signs warning
you not to enter. Rebellion as bluster in the lonely
drought, those dry nights without constellations.
Who owns what in whose memory: 'Now death
is blowing through the trees' reconstituted by rain.

A Short Tour of the Cocos Atoll

From Rumah Baru the runabout
skips over the rippling tidal sweep,
the lift & drop of the hull's skin
like the crack of a sail full blown,
dead, full blown again. We traverse
sinkholes cool with depth,
almost black, like inverted islands
set in intertidal reef,
a sub-surface map
where intensity of colour
makes do for sonar.
Ashore on Pulu Labu—
the sheet anchor claws the sand,
a few chickens idle nearby.
On the island's ocean side
I lacerate my feet on splintered coral,
collect a composite rubber sheet
from which a dozen pairs of children's
thongs have been pressed somewhere
in Indonesia, brought by the tides
& currents to Cocos. A brown booby
glides high overhead,
the humid atmosphere
muffling its call—these birds
nest on North Keeling
which is out of reach, but are treasured
by the Cocos Malays as a delicacy,
a food for which the Federal police
will often travel to Home Island
to investigate a rumoured feast.
Jeff is busy casting a net
for bait fish, he hauls
in a small school & collects
the anchor. I squirm with the fish:
they flick at my feet as I grip
the gunwale. Jeff
steers towards Pulu Kembang

& I can tell he's
checking me out—test
the weird vegetarian
who lets fish go & loves
the orange & black concertinaed
bodies of sea-slugs, who
jumps onto the reef & tows
the runabout with unnaturally long legs.
The tide's retreat is in full swing.
We anchor a couple of ks from the beach.
Mud crabs bubble just below the flat.
Stands of driftwood lurk like booby traps.
Jeff chases reef sharks in knee-deep hollows
& tries to beach them. Their black tips race
towards dry land & dart suddenly
back to the depths. They are quicker than Jeff.
We walk to the island & walk back again.
The sun devastates our skin.
We suffer mutually.
Jeff heads for deep water
& says he wants to spear the treasured green fish.
He dives like a wounded frigate
& returns with nothing.
He is popular on Home Island
& speaks with thirty years
behind him. He is not the West Islander now.
And this is how I like him.
Returning to Rumah Baru
I wonder if he's the man the Cocos Malays
have been seeing—or almost seeing—shadowing
the coconut groves. Appearing at special moments,
bringing good luck.

Lightning Tree

It's stark white in this hard
winter light. At its base
brackish water spreads like exposed film
out through marshgrass & paperbarks—
a snapped bone, it punctures the skin.
On its splintered crown
the Great Egret stretches, its knifed beak
piercing the cold blue sky—
an inverted lightning strike
fielding its wings—
a crucifix—hesitating,
as if held by a magnet,
then dropping into flight,
dragging lightning rod legs.

Tenebrae

for Tracy

You are on the verge
of a resurrection,
standing on a fragile shoreline,
erosion undermining
the limestone cliff face,
expecting to plunge suddenly
into the churning ocean.
You'd rebuild memories,
though this coastline
is always changing—a childhood
hiding place eroded,
an overhang collapsed
like the tide. Those
limestone columns
reaching towards a god
that would take your past
as if it were an offering.
But though the lights
one by one extinguish
as you explore deeper,
that final light—the sun—
grows stronger,
despite the coming winter,
the darkening seas.

Wild Radishes

Across the dark fields the family is spread
While overhead the sky is haunted,
In the dull light they scour the crop
Never looking up as the day seems to stop.
Wild radishes missed will destroy the yield—
Bills to be paid, deals to be sealed.
But the plover's refusal to lift and drop,

And the absence of crow and parrot talk,
And the immense racket as stalk rubs on stalk,
Registers somewhere deep in the soul.
And as the sun begins to uncoil—
The deep green of the wheat uneasy with light—
The golden flowers of wild radishes bite
Just before they are ripped from the soil.

Drowning in Wheat

They'd been warned
on every farm
that playing
in the silos
would lead to death.
You sink in wheat.
Slowly. And the more
you struggle the worse it gets.
'You'll see a rat sail past
your face, nimble on its turf,
and then you'll disappear.'
In there, hard work
has no reward.
So it became a kind of test
to see how far they could sink
without needing a rope
to help them out.
But in the midst of play
rituals miss a beat—like both
leaping in to resolve
an argument
as to who'd go first
and forgetting
to attach the rope.
Up to the waist
and afraid to move.
That even a call for help
would see the wheat
trickle down.
The painful consolidation
of time. The grains
in the hourglass
grotesquely swollen.
And that acrid
chemical smell
of treated wheat
coaxing them into
a near-dead sleep.

Echidna

for Jacques Derrida

Rhythmically burrowing up on the toproad
in the graded remainders, the swampy contours
that look good for digging, that you'd
like to get amongst and smell—
those substrata, more than dirt and roots,
rhizomic agendas of the feeble-eyed,
uttering up refrains from where
compactness and density
are demarcation and territory,
where decaying mallee root
or corpse of storm-felled wandoo
tan the leathery bag of muscled fluid,
the flow of ants as white as Moby Dick,
as determined against the pulpy hull of trees
as against the gridded surface. Down where
the highway is sensed in the movement of sand-
particles, the *hérisson—istrice* in Italian,
in English, hedgehog—excavates
determinedly. At risk, this bristling heart
litters the roads with dedication,
symbols of the national psyche
left to bloat in the sun's blistering
prosody: *inseparation* that mimes
mechanics on the surface: *<by heart>*,
that without footnotes is still recognised
as the source of all under-movings.
I consider as memory tracking an echidna
with a farmer in 'Jam Tree country'—
locating the spirit of place,
as if its being curled in a tree hollow
might validate the vast spread
of open tillage—but struck
by a kind of amnesia we wandered
in a circle tight as a fist, exhuming
the deeply choric question of rendering
our meanderings into prose,

into idle chatter to accompany
a few beers in the pub that night;
the portfolio of our imagined data
presented with detachment
as the slow-moving underminer
of our confident lyrical selves
fed ravenously,
deep in the heart
of the forest.

The Hunt

for Les Murray

A bounty of 'fame throughout the district and no
chores for a week' was placed on The Tiger by my
      Uncle. We'd all seen it
      plenty of times over
the years—a huge beast that came down from the Top Bush
and raided the chicken coop, took the guinea fowl,
      and slaughtered pets. It was
a true feral, begotten by ferals. It was,

in a sense, a species entire in itself.
Those many sightings over the years of a 'large
      predator' we put down
      to The Tiger. It seemed
like a joke of nature—green-grey fur with musty
yellow waves running like stripes down its flanks, massive
      jaw with steel teeth that shone
as it snarled in a spotlight before vanishing

into the bush. For two years it had been hunted—
even the local pro fox shooter couldn't bring
      home its scalp. One winter
      holidays my cousin
and I packed our tent and kit, shouldered arms and crossed
into the scrub. Deep into the dark forbidding
      foliage we plunged. We struck
      camp close to the centre
of the island of wandoo and mallee, a large

copse surrounded by florescent green crops of wheat.
At dusk we shot three grey rabbits as they emerged
      from their warrens. It was
      quick and nothing was said.
Placing them in a damp hessian sack we spent hours
traipsing through the bush by torchlight, dragging the sack
      behind us. The scent spread,

we emptied the corpses
on a patch of open ground and set to digging

hollows and laying traps—fierce iron jaws decayed
by rust, straining beneath sand-covered newspaper
      disguising the ambush.
      We took turns in laying
them, one holding the torch, the other spiking chains
into dirt, bracing springs with a boot. The traps ringed
      the offering. Rubbing
the ground with a corpse we masked our sharp scent before

casting it back on the pile. The cold bit at our
bones. Finished, we didn't linger—a strange fear took
      hold of us and something
      nudged its way under our
confidence. We returned to the campsite. Morning
was bitter—tamarisks were heavy with frost, sheathed
      with rapiers of ice.
      We struggled with a fire,
ate by the smouldering, eye-stinging hearth. Rifles

in hand we made our way to the place. *The Altar
of the Dead* one of us muttered without humour.
      The Tiger was there. Dead—
      frozen solid. The stripes
on its flanks blurred by the dark matting of fur. Three
of the traps had snatched its limbs; the others had been
      triggered and lay beaten
nearby. The Tiger had chewed off its trapped forepaw

which lay half-digested in the trap's maw, back legs
stretched as if by some medieval torturing
      device. The carcasses
      of the rabbits had not

been touched. We buried them with The Tiger; buried
the traps, deep. We packed our gear and went home, telling
       Uncle that The Tiger
       would never be caught, that
it was a creature not of this world—a bitter
cold had struck our bones, fire bringing no relief.

An Aerial View of Wheatlands in Mid-Autumn

'Indeed, it is a question if the exclusive reign of this orthodox beauty is not approaching its last quarter.'
—Thomas Hardy, *The Return of the Native*

In the reciprocity of summer
And the year's first frosts, the green eruption
Hesitant, the stramineous remainder
Of last season's crop converts to nitrogen
As slowly overhead the spotter plane
Dissects the quickening flesh of Wheatlands,
The probing eye of the camera hidden
From your curious surveillance, while stands
Of mallee gnaw at the salty badlands.

They will offer to sell you the stolen
Moment, the frozen minutiae of your
Movement within the tableau, the tension
Extracted with such unwanted exposure:
The screams of the cockatoo, the tractor
Aching deep in its gut having swallowed
A brace of teeth as it crunched into gear,
Bleats of sheep on their way to be slaughtered,
The drift as a neighbour sprays weedicide.

Remember though that if given the chance
You would scrutinize someone else's yard,
So it may be worth adjusting your stance
In the light of such a double standard.
Forget that the land looks scarred and tortured:
That call for order in the rural scene,
For Virgil's countryside satiated
With weighty corn and Campanian wine,
And consumed by olives and wealthy swine,

Is not the harmony of this decade.
Instead look to the flux of soil and fire,
The low loping flight of the darkest bird,
The frantic dash of the land-bound plover,

The breaking of salt by errant samphire,
The flow of water after steady rain,
The everlasting in bright disorder,
The stealthy path of the predating plane
Cutting boundaries as you sow your grain.

A Bright Cigar-Shaped Object Hovers Over Mount Pleasant

It starts in the park near Brentwood Primary School
and moves rapidly towards Mount Pleasant
a bright cigar-shaped object that darts
and jolts across the demarcation lines
of class that aren't supposed to exist in Australia
but do because even Labor voters prefer
to be on the Mount Pleasant side of the divide
if for no other reason than it pushes property
prices up. It follows the line of my escape-
route from school, the same route a man
without a face in a dark car crawls along,
calling to me as I break into a run,
the car door opening and a clawed hand
reaching out to drag me in, the cigar-
shaped object stopped stock still
and hovering like the sun, hovering
as if it's always been in that spot, always
been overhead, as hot as hell despite
the cold setting in, the sweat emanating
from my forehead, the light bright in my eyes.

Dispossession

protection
aggravated
destruction
Almighty
construction
proclamation
probability
autonomy
disease
species
autonomy
links
quality
vis-à-vis
the centralised
London dealer in native art
landing
like something out of songlines
the press
commission/s
traditional
punishments
appropriate
authentic
threads
heresy
controls
white hunters
alcohol
abuse
custody
motivating
sit-down
leaders
nominated
by
mining companies

pastoral leases
progressive
impacts
and sustain
extinguishment!
as assistance
modifies acts
presence
traces
the local
and maintains
representatives
authentic
claims
to constitutional
strategy
faith
and disobedience
and wicked
tears
conferring
tame
forms
of ownership
rifles
revisionist
histories: lights
in the sky
shackles

Figures in a Paddock

In their wake the furrows,
partings in long grass,
burrs hell-darning their socks
like recovered memories.

Parallel to the fence—star pickets
mark depth, interlock mesh
letting the light and visuals
through, keeping the stock

in or out—like religious tolerance.
Down from the top-road to the creek,
arms akimbo, driven against
insect-noise, a breeze that should

be rustling up a performance.
Towards the dry bed, marked
by twists and shadow-skewed
rivergums, bark-texture

runs to colour like bad blood.
The sky is brittle blue,
foliage thin but determined:
colour indefinable beyond green.

They walk, and walking makes history.
And tracks. All machinery.
The paddock inclines. A ritual of gradients.
Ceremony. Massacre. Survey.

Funeral Oration
for Joyce Heywood

The grave is a gate you send flowers through,
and the pink blossom frosting the northern hemisphere
is, on closer observation, a confluence of species.
There is a scent that's as much about lingering
as leaving, and it's about time the ploughs
were moving down there. The geographical
centre fluctuates while the magnetic centre
remains rock solid. Prayer goes somewhere
and is not lost and expects nothing back.
An old tree—a York gum—oozes sap
like it's something special in this genealogy.
Most of the family is there and words are said
and those who can't attend wait for news of the dead
       as now it is all about memory.

Hectic Red

Quartz sparks randomly
on the pink and white crust
of the salt flats, spread out
beyond the landing,
where bags of grain—
wheat and oats
in plastic and hessian—
lips sewn shut,
packed tight, flexing dust
and dragging their feet
to the edge, are tipped
onto the truck—feed-
grain, filling out
the flattop, another body sack
waiting to be fed,
from top to bottom,
the sheep hollow-gutted
in the long dry, green-feed
deficient and this
the diminishing stock
of back-up tucker;
the best paddocks
up beyond the salt
all hoofed and bitten,
stray tufts targeted
and levelled,
dry roots crumbling
and dropping to dried-out
stream-beds beneath,
so no new encrustations
of salt emerge back down
in the low places, just the old crust,
pinking off—at night,
the crazy pick-ups
spinning wheels
and throwing headlights,
the bonnets rising and falling

in choppy waves, the light
as unstable as a camera
and the darkness dropping in
like black sacking; bleak rabbits
dashing about,
their blood infra,
the forecast—hectic red.

Sine qua non

Those apples I've struggled to write
for years—lines about cooking
and fermentation and decoration:
haphazard globes denting as they crash
to the path, tepid in the first days
of autumn, enjambed like invocation—
of days apart, polished by humidity.
The collapsing moment: the thrill
of encounter, the sticky fluid
of memory spread like a blemish.
Those stray trees untended
glower like wild planetariums:
a pleasure I'd neglect, brought
so close to you, here in the past.

The Burning of the Hay Stacks

'Laved in the flame as in a Sacrament . . .'
   —Thomas Merton

There was a rash of burnings
that autumn—the arson squad
said circumstances were suspicious,
but there was a lack of evidence
to pursue a prosecution.

Always at evening, in heavy weather,
humidity insisting something happen.
Storms came later, but there was no lightning
to blame. And the pattern pushed
the odds out of orbit: with a bit

of imagination, you could make five
points with the town as the centre.
Pentacle, Pentecost, pent-up energy.
The wick lit, they just erupted,
traces of sap crackling like trees

rundown by bushfire. At a point
above the stacks a blue halo, wavering
circle that looped down over the last light
of days just not right for seeding.
On the fifth occasion, the owners

of one property called on the Anglican
minister to do a blessing, and then, for good
measure, the Catholic priest. An old Aunt
suggested looking back into the Old
Testament, talking persistently

about Jerusalem belonging to all religions,
of plagues and desert and exile,
her long-dead husband's Jewish roots
lost to the fires, the hidden fuel
that feeds the burning of haystacks.

Chainsaw

The seared flesh of wood, cut
to a polish, deceives: the rip and tear
of the chain, its rapid cycling
a covering up of raw savagery.
It is not just machine. In the blur
of its action, in its guttural roar,
it hides the malice of organics.
Cybernetic, empirical, absolutist.
The separation of Church and State,
conspiracies against the environmental
lobby, enforcement of fear, are at the core
of its modus operandi. The cut of softwood
is deceptive, hardwood dramatic: just
before dark on a chill evening
the sparks rain out—dirty wood,
hollowed by termites, their digested
sand deposits, capillaried highways
imploded: the chainsaw effect.
It is not subtle. It is not ambient.
It is trans nothing. A clogged airfilter
has it sucking up more juice—
it gargles, floods, chokes
into silence. Sawdust dresses boots,
jeans, the field. Gradually
the paddock is cleared, the wood
stacked in cords along the lounge-room wall.
A darkness kicks back and the cutout
bar jerks into place, a distant chainsaw
dissipates. Further on, some seconds later,
another does the same. They follow
the onset of darkness, a relay of severing,
a ragged harmonics stretching back
to its beginning—gung-ho,
blazon, overconfident. Hubristic
to the final cut, last drop of fuel.

180 Degrees of Separation

The sheep came here before entering the yard
for the killing: he would cut their throats

with a short, worn knife. I have written
about this in a variety of ways. I keep

rewriting the same poem. But there were
many occasions I witnessed—the word's

appropriate—and a book entirely composed
of poems about sheep killing would not

be enough. Maybe a line for each organ?
A page for each carcass? A section for the skins

laid out over the fence—oily and yellow inside.
The wool shorn back to the uncoloured outer skin

Month after month. Years. Decades.
He kept the freezer full of sheep parts.

I'm sure he didn't enjoy what he did—it was work.
He noted the pigs enjoyed the innards

dumped from the barrow. The cold brought
steam, the heat a stink that permeated.

An outdoor task—below the shed overhang—
for all weathers. The frightened bleat like a storm.

What I've not considered is the shape
of the paddock where the sheep selected for killing

waited out their time. Only a few, the feed
was rarely under pressure. A triangular paddock,

its angles went from relatively open to suffocation.
The sheep, I recollect, rarely grazed in the narrow

point—the angle furthest away from the killing yard
and slaughter hook. They moved on trails looped

across the broad end of the field, the end nearest the dirt
with its red inside red: like oil-stains that go a long way

below the surface, sit on the water table. Float.
I wonder if the shape of the paddock was coincidence

or convenience: the mathematics of bottlenecks
and imperative, the sides always adding up: the half-life,

the lifting out of the herd: there is no random
gesture in the killing, and the prejudice

is lost as good people grow used to it.
Forgive them Lord, they know not what they do?

Rodeo

Ay-o-rodeo, hooray!
  Rodeo, rodeo, yay!
    Some say it will stay
    Even when they
Cart it far away, far away!

Wheel-less, it bogs down in clay,
  Leafy suspension dismay,
    Rust in the chassis
    Motor antsy,
The tray-top of the Rodeo

Is sieve-like, the Rodeo's
  tray-top is sieve-like. Hooray
    Ay-o-rodeo,
    Hey, rodeo!
A long way from the factory.

All about the enamelled
  Body, tufts of cape tulip
    Lash and flurry, strip
    Economy
Those robots in the factory.

O rodeo, Rodeo,
  Rodeo, rodeo, O,
    Under crow gestalt,
    Not far from salt,
We praise your brand-name, your shattered

Windows; the silver trimmings
  Stripped to the name Rodeo,
    Mauvaise foi, as your
    Aerial claws
The smoky air, rodeo!

Once we whipped you up into
  A lather, a glint in your
    High beam, those burn-outs
    We used to tout
At crossroads, Rodeo, a show!

Ay-o-rodeo, hooray!
  Rodeo, rodeo, yay!
    Some say it will stay
    Even when they
Cart it far away, far away!

The Damage Done

Someone is revving the shit out of a chainsaw;
We look up from flatlands to the wooded summit,
Up past the hillside paddocks, up at the place of law.

Policemen don't go there, it's not their law,
Whitegums cast no shade over sheep, roots of wattle vibrate,
Someone is revving the shit out of a chainsaw.

After the heatwave, vandals cut wood like straw,
The damage done out of sight, we hear them harvest into night,
Up past the hillside paddocks, up at the place of law.

Tomorrow, in extrovert morning light, it will be hard to ignore
Their lines of light, ghosts of the outcrop trapped in granite,
Someone is revving the shit out of a chainsaw.

Night birds stuck in raw, dark air, left to claw
Phantoms and microwaves, asides in the script,
Up past the hillside paddocks, up at the place of law.

Down here, the parrots have returned—there are more
Than we thought. They scan for seed out of habit.
Someone is revving the shit out of a chainsaw,
Up past the hillside paddocks, up at the place of law.

Among the murk I will find things to worship

Among the murk I will find things to worship,
the memory dressed up in acrylics, dawn-
haze training scrub on the mountain, bird-exchange
        tossed up around them.

That probity will move independently
rocks the river red gum, roots set down below
the salt line, a monoplane grinding the air,
        droning tepid clouds.

Christ, down-wind, picks up the static, facing us—
offers least resistance; down in the city
we eat with the Buddhists, admire the Jewish
        critic in traffic.

Amid she-oaks the Prophet stirs the thornbill,
the galahs cut their jagged about-face flight,
rust and oily residue slick the river,
        and yet, deny them!

The old man has lost his farm, moved into town—
huddles in the kitchen, Metters Stove burning
low, rubs the emblem from his tractor's bonnet,
        calling heaven down.

My father has never been to America

My father has never been to America
but when I think America I think of him—
a life in Kenworth trucks, admiration
for the company reps flown down
to show them how to do it for Australia.

My father sticks with the government
because they're keeping things pretty much the same;
he thinks gridiron's a dickhead's game
and Bud is like drinking urine,
but otherwise it's America all the way.

My mother has been to America
and likes to speak other languages.
She recognises English is not the only way.
She constantly tries to vote out right-wing
governments, and though fearing the police,

thinks it's good the protesters
peacefully stand up to the evil empire.
She admires the politeness, not the policing.
My mother and father divorced
when I was seven—my mother
worshipped Elvis, my father didn't.

Peonies, 105 Brooklyn Street, Gambier, Ohio

These peonies being like nothing else,
we have only the word itself—or conveyance
of the storm, location, centrifuge of sparklers
wrapped in crinoline, synthetic flowers
my grandmother used to style for shows
of the flourishing;
                                    tossed up in green plumage,
coeval with blood red or eye-white, contesting
the blue covering of carbon and green plastic
black on the edge that keeps the tomato seed
of an earlier season from rejoining the soil,
tossing up a fruit to parody peonies
in lush despoiling, ragged in pile-driving rain,
bereft of prayers of adoration
that makes sentience bearable;
                                    I tug a splash
of colour like a banner across my going,
to forget the mower cutting down
the spears of asparagus until the crowns
are dry while the ground is sodden, these vegetable
contradictions when the village encloses,
refuses to let you out no matter how far from peonies
you leave your calling-cards:
                                    those remembered flowerings
steeped in emblems and perfumes, as blank
as someone else's ribbons won
before you were born, colour fading
tantamount to facilitating sparrows and robins,
as rare as the imprint of iris,
each to his own, hanging about like solar panels
in the filling dark, collecting what's not caught up
in peonies as implosive as murmur.

In Expectation of the Turkey Vulture

Make no comparisons:
involute head, shredder of routes
veined by roads thin-on or richly
temporal: the hurting prayer,
narcissistic drop when thermals
lack charisma: how can we think
of anything but war?
                                My summer
birthday back in the Avon Valley
is Groundhog Day here,
and a malignant weatherman
tells me it will always
be that way, wherever I go:
                                once here,
you've been got at.
                                The turkey vulture
flies over Gambier in summer,
picking at the dead souls
of small birds, routing
drop-ins by movie stars
and rock icons.
                                Rodents
brisk in reactive corn fields.
I can't show connection
no matter the accuracy
of observation or euphemism,
and am increasingly lost
where seasons don't meet
along rippled, disturbed edges:
carrion laid out for extraction,
and the bold bird hacking
at the corpse of *all passers-by*
as if it were yesterday.

Red Barn Truisms

1.

I read in a town a couple of hours away
and am told of a rash of barn burnings.
The barns are red, are built by many.
The barns are red, fall to a single flame.

2.

We hear of arms-caches among hay
and animals, and grey snow mutes
the response of hardy winter birds—
chickadees, nuthatches, snow buntings.

A grackle and a merlin, a rumour
and someone or something running
through the cornstalks in endless
night, snowdrifts disturbed on hills.

Home, home soon—past Big Bear
closed down car park parody of space,
emptiness. Can you tell maples,
red dogwoods and black walnuts in this?

3.

To say I did, we did, is to say it's memory.
But the great blast that killed the house,
that drove us under heaps of blankets,
baby at your breast, the river and ice

warm in his blood, your milk,
to retreat to the Inn and hold up,
to see icicles conduct epiphanies.

To see all that, to have reached out
to those who held the power.
Never to fall asleep as the body
loses hold of its temperature.

4.

Black ice slide coming home
the back way—past the house
of a thousand planted pines,
into the T-junction, a cosmopolitan
        moment of mortality.

5.

As war is made to happen I am in St Louis
and you're in Gambier with the children—
silent vigil on Middle Path, newborn
in the pram already knowing trees
will bloom, the peaceful gathering
of strength. I give a lecture on pacifism
and talk with a woman who has lost
her son before elegies of war are written.

6.

I walk along the Kokosing from Mount Vernon to Gambier
and back again with our daughter. Across the bridge, the river

lightly and gently whitewaters a bend, flatly foaming.
Splintered trees are portals. People pass and we know them slightly.

How we fit in the silence is a puzzle we won't solve.
We talk like that, walking, difficult walking. Listening

more than talking, the sun low to the horizon, lighting
the woods. At school, a teacher brands a student

on the arm in the name of God. There's that, too.

7.

Head of a deer lolling
off the backless pick-up,

less blood than you'd think.
And killing with rules

and all the rules
broken, you'd think.

8.

'I have a son in the military.'
And that's that. Whatever your politics.

9.

Painted Ladies 'munitions wealth'
where the underground railroad
ran on through—the duality or contradiction
or logical history of the 'most Republican

town in America'? On the edge of the corporation,
slow down past the bar where things are sorted out.
Or, better still, to the health-food store across from the tire store
where the Mennonite woman discusses life as it unfolds.

10.

Daniel Decatur Emmett.
'Dixie'.
Blackface.
Minstrel.
There's a sign.
Students talk about it,
So do I.

11.

A neighbour, a poet who can write
lines of American like a Roman poet,
could only have written the groundhog
climbing a tree and going out on a limb
to fall and break it. Seasonal change
was part of its prosody.

12.

Who was it offered me a red barn to write in?
I am not sure if I've got it right, but there's a vague
memory I am trying to reconstruct. A red barn
in a field of snow, of cornstalks, of edges.
There's a photo, but it might be of a different
red barn. It had lightning conductors
and dropped snow quick. Once, so far far away,
I was struck by lightning twice. There were
more than two conductors to earth truth.

Senses and the Wheatbelt

TEXTURES OF THE WHEATBELT

Hessian waterbag cool in shade-house
swings with resistance, a cooling action
of flow that would slow flight down,
interfere with logic, a textural
draught, a rough divvying up of cloth
and air and water tilted against a burnished horizon,
stems of Paterson's Curse inflicting glass needles
like beacons, to rub against the angle of entry
like cropping out of season, or setting
a rabbit-trap off with a bare foot or sandal;
the shed strips of rough grey outer bark
of the York gum tune the green-grey
glide of undercurrents, the underneaths
out of sun and weathering winds,
gripping barbed wire to pin it down
and climb over to catch the flickback and skin-jag
and to wonder why you deserve such ill luck:
it's a matter of physics; an exfoliation of rust
is sharp and withering, crumbling cut,
all damage in bind-a-twine ripping over skin,
through clenched hands as bale slips sideways
and spills in segments, a burning as fire
and satin and density of colour,
red welts rising against the pliers' cut,
so much plant fibre and wire, blood slicks
like oil and water mixed against chemistry,
a science of bone finery and sharpness,
sinew and sever, a feathery drift of ash
made ash again where fires are burnt often,
where steel is extreme even through gloves,
and a clod of loamy earth sticks just right,
too much in heavy clay, too little in sand
welling out vast planes, low scrub gone,
a white scrunch echoing rims of brackish water,
wings and carapaces irritant and emollient

on harvest windscreens, grain-dust working
pores best described as agnostic
in their receipt of itch.

SOUNDS OF THE WHEATBELT

The grasshopper roar is almost the locust roar
though not quite a swarming, just holding off
an issue of damp and dry, though intensity
of insect traffic as three-dimensionally tense
the eardrum of the paddock strains and a barking dog
is hoarse against the rustling electric scrum,
the whirr, the racket, the scratching and clicking,
attempt to flip upright, rotoring hover, Doppler
rush-by, hell-diver and sound-barrier imploder,
scissoring and slicing, smashing and crunching,
serrations pulling and parting, riffling carapaces
to expose the sound-makings, staccato
premonitions, signalling nightfall and drawn-to-lights,
heat seekers and seers of the heart's glowing beating outline,
unearthing and gnashing out to pincer
the bull by the horns, flutter as fine as the wings
that reflect the eye of the wagtail, sun's stimulation . . . wing-walking
along hotlines of nymphs and egg-layings,
feathers see-sawing down from cracked dead branches
where an arguing and jesting flock of galahs high-balls
into sunset, zips ripped down and jamming skin,
crows beak-twisting and drawing out the inevitable,
thick rustle of bobtail with just-enough acceleration
to get down below the flurry of wingsters,
incendiary consumers in a rush to get done,
such a short claim to our already accustomed ears . . .
threatening to conflagrate the crackling grasses.

Of the tongue things eaten make more words
than words make food, but that's no reason
we should succumb . . . asked at the cut-out piss-up
the shearer says taste . . . here is beer and lanolin,
blood of the sheep I shear . . . the brief
action of fire on the flensed beast . . . By slow burning
wood stoves, quick electric elements and blue gas jets,
the verdict is gravy and custard, salt and sugar,
and the ease with which a fork does or doesn't
prod the paddocks; taste is the most delusional
of senses, so many poisons sweet or inoffensive
to these multitudinous guardians of the temple
pass through undetected, so many sour tastes
prevent the absorption of essential nutrients;
dirt in mouth, toothpaste, tobacco . . . and kerosene
from the back of the hand wiped across the lips
without thinking . . . sampled 'new foods'
ancient as bland tofu enlivened by soy sauce,
'old foods' as vibrant as wild jams and seed flours,
entrepreneurial cross-pollination
of the palate and erogenous zones,
the essence of home-baked bread—
wishful thinking against bad seasons,
rainwater stored in corrugated tanks
sweetly bitter with its taint of the metallic,
paradoxes of foods stained by woodsmoke,
taste of our own sweat, cauterised longing
brought by thirst, a blank zone induced
by scalding coffee, clove oil for the toothache
too far to drive to get it seen to, parrot-torn
stone-fruit a display of prepositions as the cyanide
of the bite-down releases stickiness
and a freshness beyond the mint
held in the cheek, tractor winging it
as the wheel spins below the ball

of the hand, dust become grit
and the concreting over of buds,
a dull bridging of the salacious creeks,
salt hardening the arteries, tasting
from this far apart: bitter almonds
breathed in through the mouth.

SMELLS OF THE WHEATBELT

Yes, the smell of hay being cut when slightly damp,
that heady, intoxicating lushness, a poison
sustaining allergies and full heads; yes, the wheat
harvest, the dry stalks cut and eaten by the header,
spilled like alcohol into the field bins, trucks
overloaded for the silos—both sides of a simile;
yes, the smell of wet sheep on a frosty morning
warming rapidly, the sun blazing though far
enough away to keep the temperatures down,
the olfactories unsure as stung and bitten; the sweet
putrefaction of a field of flowering canola, the weird
anomaly of wattle bloom, the layering of dust occluding
its own mineral and cellular odour; the perfumed
corrosion of herbicides killing from the roots up,
leaf down, inside out; sting of pesticides washed
from crop to river, the chromatic gleam
filming the surface a collusion of smell and taste,
a trauma of the eye the balancing liquid
plethoric, yellow patches of cells so close to seeing
the plumes and clouds of fumes, the effusors anosmiac;
the dog having rolled in the realm of the dead,
a secret place of dumped animals, ribs
splayed and skin hanging in coagulate 'high heaven'
misrepresentation; in from labouring
over fencing, the underarm scouring
of shower and clean clothes: hedonic,
fugitive, diffuse, neutralised, abated.

If all colours therein are to be found in the spectral tail-feathers
of parrots, so are they to be found in the flickering slither
of a juvenile dugite, come into the house through an uncovered
drainpipe, working the polish of the stone-tiled floor
hard for traction, and sending shudders through the air
like a photo taken out of focus so that resonances
of the body shape unfold as an incremental halo
about its form—intentionally. In the half-light
of the corridor the translucent then opaque
olive green gives way to an under-shadow
of night-rich blackness, the ochre of its adult
manifestation a slippage between the overlap of scales,
a body stretching beneath the set weight of its skin,
a place to shelter searched out, senses hard pressed
and the thin darkness of narrow places
a rainbow dense with chemical light
of its touch, the streaming colours within.

ESP IN THE WHEATBELT

Seasonal as once their coming here
was loss or bliss or change of scenery,
such draperies or oil on foundered iron,
pot shots at dawn, or prayers
said in pepper trees or halfway
down a well, or the glass
wandering across the board, names
spelt out through fog, twitching
branches of gravel-pit fires,
wash-away paddocks a semi-landslide
on gentle slopes, yet carrying
enough 'externalisation of the senses'
to make palaver of the emotions;
cross-country she cried in recesses,
beneath sole trees in cleared spaces,
among stepped bricks of broken
and robbed houses, seeing nothing,
hearing nothing, tasting nothing,
smelling nothing, feeling nothing,
and yet the rush of dirt and blood
and the mercury dropping
below horizons, crowding
of lost or fading relatives,
hurt and pleasured and enlivened
runs and furrows, the wet 'n' dry
of a contra-spectrum, disk plough
scoring black out of white quartz agglomerations,
sub-currents sprung up like whispering
circuit boards, a wattle and daub
of storylines as resonant
as the hot kitchen, ink welling
out of the cracks in the bureau.

Sympathy—Bogged

1. FRONT VIEW

Heavy vehicle broad grin, tilted.
        Bogged—no traction.
Back wheels down to the axles.
        Bogged—no traction.
The artistry of submersion,
Barely detectable from front-
        On, dark clouds rolling overhead.
        Bogged—no traction.

2. SIDE VIEW

Sympathise—he's down on his knees.
        Bogged—no traction.
Spirit level bubble ascends.
        Bogged—no traction.
Low-geared he tries to ease it out,
Semi-grip then centrifugal
        Rip, spinning wildly, flywheel blitz.
        Bogged—no traction.

3. REAR VIEW

Deluge of Judgement—lateral.
        Bogged—no traction.
Incrementally dropping—cored.
        Bogged—no traction.
Illusion, merging verticals
And horizontals, tail-light sludge
        And embers—collapsed stars—buried.
        Bogged—no traction.

4. BIRD'S-EYE VIEW: CODA

Black-shouldered kite hovers—faint light.
        Bogged—no traction.
Frayed tow-rope stretched between red cars.
        Bogged—no traction.
Ghost figures direct the action.
The triangle shifts, breaks angle.
        Old rope conducts—red on red, mud.
        Towed out—traction.

Wave Motion Light Fixed and Finished

Light carves a surface;
Light anneals fibres;
Light reflects and polishes;
Light collects in red gums;
Light infuses the river-mouth;
Light surfs rock and sand;
Light caught outside focuses in the studio;
Light's harmonics; Light's deletions;
Light's semi-tones of shadow;
silver parcels of sky-light; panels like prayer mats;
silver-leaf leaves flattened rolled out luminous ignition of solar
panels cloud formational reprise and a top-dressing finished glance;
ergo sum, ergo sunt, ergonomics of steel-pinned beauty,
Frida Kahlo strength, the saw bench, saw-light, wound
healing as wood planed to river loop and stretch, upwind downstream
filaments of trees reaching into salt-freshwater rendition, to walk
on black foil lift-off surface tension skip a beat
fish jump in largesse of cloud, tonnage of water vapour
as carved out old laws and coastal raiders
as fourteenths of a whole, holistically challenging to float
above a bed of wood, a bed of air, a bed of light, as solid as erosion
from southerlies cutting into hamlets and guilds,
a code, a tapping of branch on branch we might think
vaguely light Morse code this small part we can see at once
of any vision, any transmutation of heightened emotion, the variable
light of idea, sketch, rough, and finished product, artefact, item, example,
distillation . . . an economy of presence, an evidence of passing through the waves
of horizon, the highs and lows of occupation . . . silver nitrate tint, Polaroid
caught out before exposure, lightning-driven . . . trees lit up like superstition,
    anatomy
interface grain reaching across planar quelling of spilt tea, spilt coffee,
blackbutt counteraction, storm-fallen revivification, as if each cell in its harmonic
is charging for renewal, the divan the ocean we slide into, nesting
chairs called back to the same spot to amplitude, sine wave
that lopes scansion bevelled edges tanged to ferrule and groove,
to sit and look out at imprints of rapture or haunting, luminous fire-wrought
hardened stock and buffer zone, delay contact consumed and melded

to carry out day-to-day activities, concentrate on one aspect of revelation,
a music emanates as light over ripples and echo-soundings
of wood density and rock density and water density and the sunset off-cuts
of light dampened, the temple stretched, this slow-time analysis of decompression,
emerging from within the element, the bends bring contract
and oxygen does something else, here the bends are absorbed, you flow
with their emergence, the night-eyes not seen as steel glints
a fine line, spirits of night falter on light borders withdrawing or creeping
into the vista, a front blown out, sleep bandwidth in the silent sound system,
the pin dropping so loud in distillation; pragmatically, light moves across the table,
pragmatically, light fills the wall behind the canvas, the floor and walls
light-heavy, light-drenched; changeable, flighty, instant, light thrills
the horizon, thrills the sharp lines
outside the halo, runs riot, and river flows on
and the furniture in the bedroom, living room, lounge room, dining room . . .
settles; going out . . . work, a show, a walk . . . a sense of where things sit
stays with you, side-step, accommodate, meld . . . as seagull, osprey, sooty
oystercatchers, criss-cross and throw up solar panels, throw up diffuse
maps of absolute light; in the land's curvature, the shark swims through
the territory of roo and wallaby, heavy-bodied cows light on their feet,
up to the river's edge, forests breathing moistly; the lamps shifts and haunted
trees emerge, or figures of the dispossessed—they can't be built out,
textured into the immensity of ocean and sky and headland,
low wattage of sunset driven up over rise, silhouette intensifying
where we walked, where all have walked out of memory,
taking sustenance out of the reconfigured picture,
having been there before and before; a line of herring
race the coastline, heavier fish sit close to the bottom, poised
on the edge of our seats, the table floats on silver air, the sky
made horizontal, the horizon a vertical line attaching
ceiling and floor—no vertigo comes with this, or searching out vertigo
it is a sonorous warmth of blended specificity: light peaking and dropping,
crests and troughs, concurrent and ecliptic,
the certainty of form when solar activity upsets the animals, confuses
bio-rhythms, the certainty of the shape waking to look out over the same space,
sunspots ripping through heath and forest, sizing canvas and coating
the hard dead growth, a form of rekindling

the ups and downs of days alone, days full of shadow, days burning with glare
and a brooding atmosphere, days becalmed, days where a memory
forced down below the surface, planes of light, bursts out
like caught sun, and then settles back into the dimensions
of the domestic, the pastoral: light transfigures, regenerates, blinds;
light is not to be taken for granted; light's properties grow
in the limestone caverns where we haven't seen, the sea connected
with where we stand, or sit, or spread ourselves out to float or hover
or petrify or sink down into surfaces below surfaces
and perspectives of light, thin membrane of land carved by seven waves
then seven waves and so on, on one side and lightly so on, on the other
more circumstantial though never casual the repetitions of wave motion,
river lappings carried against the banks against the skin-drum, against
Light's semi-tones of shadow;
Light's harmonics; Light's deletions;
Light caught outside focuses in the studio;
Light surfs rock and sand;
Light infuses the river-mouth;
Light collects in red gums;
Light reflects and polishes;
Light anneals fibres;
Light carves a surface . . .

Riding the Cobra at the York Show (The Artificial Infinite)

Hoodwinked by the flat-lining, inside out
Silver lining of every absent cloud,
A clear day halo, a vulcanised rout
Of dust and eucalypt, diesels and loud
Stereos hyping up an eager crowd:
Addendum to truck and trailer, it rears
Up and contorts, hydraulically proud,
Eyes in the back of the head, cobra peers
Out into the hills and paddocks: it fears

Less with each scream. Down there—about to wake—
Snakes that wouldn't recognise it—dugites,
Gwardars, pythons, blind snakes . . . this clap-trap take-
All-before-it blow-in whiplash that skites
Loud enough to wake the dead, deny rites
Of belonging. Still, it rouses the prey
To come out into the open, reach heights
Once unimaginable; praise this lay
Society, almost too proud to pray.

Hooked elbow, steel lap-trap, drop-pod lock-down . . .
Centrifuge of senses and kinetics,
On the blow-out, rise up and twist, your frown
Looking down and out at the granite quirks
Of sunset ridges, peripatetics
Of ripening crops, glib orality
Of sideshow clowns, unravelling antics
Of object and shade . . . the finality
Of bent guns in shooting tents, reality

Sublimated and betrayed like roos caught
In a spotlight; centre of tension, soul
Lolling out of the mouth, memory fraught
With unresolved theologies, the roll
Of light and unction dipped in the blurred bowl
Of endolymph, the body osmotic;
This sharp arabesque as elemental

As Hyperion's car freaking parrots
And judges of the show's best: despotic!

So cedillas hanging heavy with bi-
Lateral agreement, torque and sentience
Weighed up in slowing, operator's wry
Perving as limbs unfold, his dependence
On post-rush joy hidden by a grimace:
Vertigo, obtuse valley-lift anchored
By hill's reprise . . . cobra lodged in conscience,
Iron-clad alibi, convalescing, coiled
Double helix, lime-lit, reloaded—bored.

Canto of the Moths

The rains have come and winter
is not as far away as it was looking,
though beneath shadecloth

and over the glistening white sand
of Timmy's sandpit, hundreds
of moths are staggering

through the air, falling to sand
to fly up confused again. In dull
green light they are tiny angels

without entries or exits,
and following them with our eyes
we grow giddy and confused.

Their wings heavy with rain,
dust is running off like sludge.
The terrace of sand a desert

of the drowning and drowned.
Plastic buckets and shovels,
rakes and rubber balls,

compact earth-movers and bulldozers,
starfish and castles, all tombstones
where there should be no markers

of the real. In a place where shadows
filter through shadecloth onto sand,
late rains have altered the rules:

angels, like spent nuclear fuel,
toxify in their different forms,
boomerang back into sacred lands.

Canto of All Birds Celestial

All birds celestial, moving through purgatorial
vapours, ascending from trees glowing gold,
bands of colour in their wings, arising from earth

itself, interlopers calling the surveyed area
of flyover 'our property'—cutting across cornices,
levels, layers, circles, rings—the list is held

by a magnet to the fridge, 'birds seen on our . . .':
black-faced cuckoo shrike, pink and grey galah,
ring-necked parrot, kookaburra, blue fairy-wren,

sacred kingfisher, rainbow bee-eater, crow,
willy wagtail, black-shouldered kite, nankeen
kestrel, wedge-tailed eagle, peregrine falcon

(telegraph lines on front road), mountain duck,
white-faced heron, black cockatoo, little corella,
Senegal dove, silvereye, rufous songlark,

jacky winter, pardalote, goshawk, swift,
golden whistler, pallid cuckoo, magpie lark,
red wattlebird, New Holland honeyeater,

crested shrike-tit, white-breasted robin, grey
fantail, weebill, yellow-rumped thornbill, painted
quail, red-capped robin, magpie, zebra finch,

Pacific heron, egret, butcherbird . . . flying
from seven trees of gold on the crest, shedding
seven bands of colour, perched on star pickets,

twists of barbed wire, alighting wild oats,
severing fruit, scratching gravel, shaking down
jam trees, earthing the aerial, infusing undergrowth.

Bushfire Sun

Howard Taylor

Smoke clouds thickens diffuses palls chokes spreads plumes swarms smothers
Smothers swarms plumes spreads chokes palls diffuses thickens clouds smoke
Smoke clouds thickens diffuses palls chokes spreads plumes swarms smothers
Smothers swarms plumes spreads chokes palls diffuses thickens clouds smoke
Smoke clouds thickens diffuses palls chokes spreads plumes swarms smothers
Smothers swarms plumes spreads chokes palls diffuses thickens clouds smoke
Smoke corona radiance halo haze   haze halo radiance corona smoke
Smoke corona radiance halo   halo radiance corona smoke
Smoke corona radiance   radiance corona smoke
Smoke corona   Orange   corona smoke
Smoke   hue of the Planckian locus   smoke
Smoke corona   Orange   corona smoke
Smoke corona radiance   radiance corona smoke
Smoke corona radiance halo   halo radiance corona smoke
Smoke corona radiance halo haze   haze halo radiance corona smoke
Smothers swarms plumes spreads chokes palls diffuses thickens clouds smoke
Smoke clouds thickens diffuses palls chokes spreads plumes swarms smothers
Smothers swarms plumes spreads chokes palls diffuses thickens clouds smoke
Smoke clouds thickens diffuses palls chokes spreads plumes swarms smothers
Smothers swarms plumes spreads chokes palls diffuses thickens clouds smoke
Smoke clouds thickens diffuses palls chokes spreads plumes swarms smothers

The Travelling Eye—a piece of "op. cit."

on Bridget Riley's "Nineteen Greys"

'The eye can travel over the surface in a way parallel to the way it moves over nature. It should feel caressed and soothed, experience frictions and ruptures, glide and drift. One moment, there will be nothing to look at and the next second the canvas seems to refill, to be crowded with visual events.'

—Bridget Riley

grey grey grey grey grey grey grey grey grey grey grey grey
grey grey grey grey grey grey grey grey grey grey grey grey
grey grey grey grey grey grey grey grey grey grey grey grey
grey grey grey grey grey grey grey **grey** grey grey grey grey
grey grey grey grey **grey** grey **grey** grey grey grey grey grey
grey grey grey grey **grey** **grey** **grey** grey grey grey grey grey
grey grey grey grey Print moves not eye.   grey grey grey grey
grey grey grey grey Print elides nature.   grey grey grey grey
grey grey grey grey Print warps green ovals grey grey grey grey
grey grey grey grey **grey** and multiplies, grey grey grey grey
grey grey grey grey **grey** drained to grey. grey grey grey grey
grey grey grey grey grey **grey** grey **grey** grey grey grey grey
grey grey grey **grey** grey **grey** **grey** grey grey grey grey grey
grey grey grey grey **grey** **grey** grey grey grey grey grey grey
grey grey grey grey **grey** Bend and twist grey grey grey grey
grey grey grey grey **grey** far to faint edges, grey grey grey grey
grey grey grey **grey** Eye stuck to surface. grey grey grey grey
grey grey grey grey Eye drained and satiate. grey grey grey grey
grey grey grey grey Eye crowds mad to centre. grey grey grey grey
grey grey grey grey grey grey **grey** grey grey grey grey grey
grey grey grey grey grey grey grey grey grey grey grey grey
grey grey grey grey grey grey grey grey grey grey grey grey
grey grey grey grey grey grey grey grey grey grey grey grey
grey grey grey grey grey grey grey grey grey grey grey grey

The Many Moods of Marilyn Monroe, à la Andy Warhol (c 1962)

1.

Solemn as stony
enclaves closed with evening;
late light lingering.

2.

Your eyes adjusting
to her eyes so accustomed
to ideas of night.

3.

So! Razzle-dazzle
spotlight enfilade colour
splash in the tabloids.

4.

The sickness is more
than her publicist lets on;
she eats oranges.

5.

That guy has *brought out*
the devil in her—who would
have thought—that nice girl!

6.

Sing Happy Birthday
Mr President and you'll
embarrass myself?

7.

Monochrome is light
and interior shading—
this is who she was?

8.

I love this goddess—
I have seen her in the fields
the wide world over.

9.

We all have off-days
when a kiss lingers longer
than a bold kisser.

10.

'Cool' requires this.
You've got to have starting points.
She deserves better.

Burning Eyes

Burning eyes that peer out of a dry crop at night,
shape the seasons and our response—
twin sparks that light the driest stalks
fail to flame, won't combust where you pass.

I see them each night driving home, lit up
by headlights—fox, cat, a rare marsupial
frozen between rows, magnetised by the car's approach.
So frequent over the last fortnight that a pall

of doubt has gripped me: an afterimage I carry
from that first encounter, reigniting in time,
same point every night. I can't bring myself to vary
the plan, to alter the variables; the scheme

of sight, of shine and glint, has trapped
us both. The dry is drying out towards harvest.
Not a vestige of moisture in the stalks—either way,
burning eyes will pass out, lack fuel to conflagrate.

Something must break. I will go away before night
comes to pass as day, or day eats far into night
with burning eyes that peer out of a dry crop.
It's the eclipse of content where compulsion stops.

Hyperbole

Patois of the shredder,
shoddy skinner, demi-
pruner of roadside vegetation.
Poète engagé, ha! I pursue data,
inform my protest,
wrest lyrics from the brutal,
but the name of this rotator,
psychopathic cutter,
is hidden, encoded.

Travelling, I have caught
its progress, high-pitched
whirring, nerve destroyer,
too often—a seasonal
assignation, slasher
moment from which
the ghost-self emerges
tattered as living
and dead flesh mixed.

Truth is, I know
the operators, know
the work they crave: a call,
a few hours, a shire
pay-cheque. Just enough.
Today we flayed the garden.
At smoko we ribbed and jibed,
exaggerated the assets
of celebrities.

Mostly, that cutting whirr.
Mostly, the screeching banshee.
Mostly, the screaming ab-dabs
this machine induces.
Short-tempered
with the kids. I hear
this—it is said among friends.
For their sakes, also,
I protest, *poète engagé*, ha!

Holus-Bolus

The whole bolus of the pocket moon
in the quadrant where I tune
paths through high grass, fire risk,
set alight by friction—boot-frisk.

Need no infrared, no day by night,
just as termites thread de-light,
owls consume mice, sacks of bone,
draw the open ground, mowed zone.

That harvest man, that mower man,
odour of cut and petrochemical tan,
to swoop across the map's day-night
spread, shadows unravelling light.

Mistletoe hang-dog meteorite,
burn up with blue butterflies bright
as all get up, or snakes and blue-
tongues out and about, so too

flyers too quick to identify. Risible.
Goose-egg nest of oats, stressed oval
mowed over without breaking,
not a crack though black veins aching

against the china-white.

Reverse Anthropomorphism

These birds—western flyeaters—are sizing
me up, making me within their own image,
moi-même, at least for the purpose of hunting.
Through glass, I watch them target their prey,
insects in the temporal zone of the verandah:

one flyeater darts out to seize an insect flyer,
then returns to watch his companion do the same.
The whole time they both keep an eye on me. *Moi-même.*
I connect with them in no way. No displacement
to fill the page: no female pushing a pram

full of letters, "protecting the male". Empirically,
they are male *and* female. It seems they perform
the *same* tactics, the same roles when hunting. Role-play?
Who am I to say? Some *would* say it's a matter
of knowing what to look for. *Moi-même.*

This is not a rare experience, it happens most days.
We have grown familiar. Don't mistake my indifference
for their indifference, or their relaxation
for a reflection of mine. We do not share.
Though I am touched that they are near.

And they manage to get done what they
need to get done. It's rich pickings
near where I sit, separated by the glass window,
insects making their own conversations,
losing lives. *Moi-même.* Role-play.

Write-off

Night drives home are always fraught
and an eye has to be kept out for kangaroos
and even emus, sometimes foxes and often rabbits
plus owls and tawny frogmouths that swoop
across the parabola of headlights. For a lifetime
I've avoided striking anything large on this road,
though the car grille has choked on insects, has glutted
with plague-season locusts. Picking wrecked bodies
from filaments of radiator, even mangled into one body
with many more legs than genetically encoded, you realise
how large each death will always be. But it seems easier
to forget about than a medium-sized death when windscreen
catches tawny frogmouth and deflects into pitch-black sheets
hung between trees that bleed a phosphorescent orange,
mimesis of the car's disturbing aura, sentinels to body-
counts not added up when cars pass in morning light,
maybe night's carcasses already lifted by foxes
and carted off to veiled dens. This calibrating
of death obsesses you driving home late, keeping
owl-eyes sharp; is shattered when a grey kangaroo
bounds straight out at high speed from the forest;
you swerve to put the balance right and it's there again,
in front of you, a temporal anomaly that slows
world down to words—'Brace! We're going to hit!'—
followed by impact, radiator meeting fan, fragmenting
into manifold and grinding out valves, cylinders —
flip of carcass past windscreen, over curve of roof,
into the aftermath of passing, wake of darkness, a sickly
tail-lit epilogue of care and obsession. What *are* prayers
really worth to the damaged, to the dead? Prayer is only
about the living, out there, out here, where death is the *only*
conversation. And to glide, brakeless, steering gone,
into an amorphous aloneness, an accident that could go
from bad to worse. To halt without order, without hope,
the car a write-off for what it's worth. And then out
of silence, shots fired in the forest, roos driven out
to escape hunters. Spotlights and dogs that chase

glimmers of eye-light in darkest dark. I know *that* dark—
it's *different,* and fear gives it no special name. I ask
my daughter to lie low in the back of the wreck—
young women can't be seen where there's no escape—
and I try to flag down a passing car. None stops,
intermittent as they are, but I am grateful the hunters
haven't emerged from the forest to check things out. A guy
with dreadlocks pulls up in a truck and relays a message
for help. In dark silence I wait with my daughter—we wait
and listen for roos' heartbeats, for the echo of the dead roo's
heart against shots fired in the dark. I tell her that my childhood
was loud with the pounding of roo hearts, that harm
doesn't mean harm will follow, and that belief works
faster than prayer. Help arrives. We push the wreck
off into a ditch as hunters emerge alert to a frisson
of life in death, mingling of metal and flesh. Spotlights
shine down on the wreck, on rescuers, on us. They rev engines
in triumph, ignoring roo hearts—small, medium-
sized, and large—beating rapidly about us, about them;
louder and brighter than engines, than spotlights.

Yellow

Tim has been filed
in Yellow Faction
at school. He is frustrated
and angry: he wants to be in
Red Faction, especially for the Cross Country,
which even five year olds train for in the Bush.
Character building. Robust. Preparatory.
I take him out to the garden
where I have piled the spent broad-bean stalks,
grey ropes of pea vines,
dead clumps of wild oats,
for a quick burning-off. We are
making ash for the next generation,
I tell him. The fire whips about in the cold
late autumn easterly. It should cut apart
the flames but incites them. Tim,
analytical as always, notes the colour of flame
and distance of colour from the fuel. The orange
and yellow flames furthest away, linger longer,
waver. I say: see, yellow is fast,
and yellow is the colour of the sun,
it is the body of the flames, orange
is the colour of the sun, it is the body
of flames. But Tim is also suspicious
of orange. When he hears a slow ballad
sung in French by, say, Piaf, he says: I don't
like it, it makes me see orange in my head.
He and I, from a distance, consider
the waverings of orange and yellow. He
interrupts the burn-down—smoke making day
night, and wisps of ash fluttering about
like something good—and says: fire
is red too and red is a great colour,
and the flames closer to what's burning
are almost blue. Blue is the fastest colour.
Inside the sun is the blue of our souls.

All other colours are fed by blue
and it makes us fast.
                    A few days ago,
during a sun shower, Tim said that rain drops
don't let some colours of the spectrum
through. Or even let them exist, like indigo,
which *must* be in the fire too.

Wattle

Every year the bright
tremor of wattle,
yellow light
yellow rattle

of stamens and pollen,
collective memory
blocking-in
understory.

This profusion
of a short-lived galaxy
provokes effusion
and heresy:

choking drought,
whirl of gases,
clearer's rout,
godless

astronomers;
neither good nor bad
can come of it: it lures
us into sacred

utterances: confess
the yellow light
is not bright
enough, or stress

the yellow light
is too bright,
far too bright
for our limited sight.

Maralinga

Hell is hollow, a gesture in a flat surface lipped in, the curve upturned—no same point if you keep going in the same direction; convex lore coated longer than words and longer than belief. A weeping tree in flower, a minuscule tree among the saltbush and deceased. A camel skeleton hunched big-boned against the track. Spirit-killer? It's a weapon they'd test a few times at least. Watson siding as water only here was apertured into lexical theft, before and after, to make the big bang, negate and relegate the gathering tribes—a plan—atomic warfare against a people so old they brought fear to investors in peerage, shock wave propelling the train slightly faster once out of Watson, where the first flock of birds seen since yesterday overfly warning markers, pink and grey galahs their chests shields worn in the x-ray rooms, all nature is conflated in the atom and there's no half-life of logic to ward off the insecurities. Clear sky thunder. The name retains. A given name. A Christian name. Exposure to the energy source of God by any sectarian configuration. Mirage of treed islands run blue, like a leak from the sky, blue blood shining over the expanse. Seriously, that's what you see: a spreading blue across the Axminster texture of the plain, as they would envisage it. Still holding the data, using it not an end in itself, down the track. That line of hills to the north. What do they hold back on the edge of the plain, the hollow bones.

Blue-ringed Octopi

To hunt shores at night evokes a word we lack:
as *greater* frustrates the *lesser,* both having deadly
bacterial bites: the painless nip that makes paralysis
look inward though wide awake, watching your
tranquillity of demise. This isn't purely fact
collated from texts, but first-hand news: hand
touching the hand that touches the skin and agitates
a calm rockpool near mangroves to rings of bright
blue that mesmerise: liquid eyes of peacock tails.
Dying mixes metaphors, lays you out flat on the sand.
Welded mouth-to-mouth. Twenty-four hours,
a single breath. Not a breath to be had outside
the host's, breathless you give nothing back.
A marriage against convention and Nature.
That's your brother at twelve saying, 'Watch it move!',
flattened swirls across needles and jags of rock,
eight small legs that collect a space to hold
the pulsing head. Inkless inscription warning
small boys it will strike fingers through water
bending with the sun. Blue wedding rings.
And waiting for an electric shock that never
manifests, to pass through body unto body,
my pulling him away to break the shock.
You rarely feel the bite. And too late
if you do, as there's no cure but breath.
And repeated in cold southern waters, where
the *lesser* lurks in bottles and shells, neat beak
that rips a tiny crab apart, vacuuming flesh. The swell
incites rockpools, and tides bring on the scuttle.
To treasure such poisons—tetrodotoxin, maculotoxin—
the child who picks over innocence, loves risk,
loves fear, half-lulled by the ravaging of that great
amnion, the ocean. Or surrounded by mangroves
up north where it's hot and putrid and salty, where

infection sets into the smallest cut—mangroves'
false sense of security, mudflats stretching out as far
as tides can ever go—blue-ringed octopi lying low
in brine tepid with waiting. Hungry but shy.

Megamouth Shark

Should we be grateful they're not claiming
it as art, but as science? Or are they smugly
doubling up—the art of preservation the boon
of research? Megamouth, so rare it wasn't recorded
as science until 1976, day-time deep dweller
off the continental shelf to rise at night to a lesser
depth, to graze screeds of plankton we barely
register? So much for autonomy and agency
in the great body of water. Megamouth, 'rescued'
from death in shallows to depthless formalin, embalmed
within stainless steel tank-of-the-dead, necropolis
aquarium so shiny and technical, with portholes
for us to peer through, its saucer eyes staring out
with a vision we can't configure, though the designer
can. The electric pump to keep preservative circulating
is eternal as power and its grid, as the toxic ocean
pulsing in the harbour. New centrepiece of the maritime
museum, its sails parsing the stiff sea breeze. Comparisons
are fuel for the patronising, and I can't help but think
this tank and its inhabitant are prescient fulfilment
of *Dune*, a pox on emperor houses of curators
and scientists, this Guild Navigator the benign
encapsulation of Edric shrouded in orange gas,
so distorted to outside eyes, plotting the courses of ships
through space without collision, devastation like anchor
lines and fishing nets, incidentals that make evidence
for our bemusement that such a beast could go unnoticed.
It offends us. There's agony in its scanning eye, its tiny
filtering teeth set in that gaping mouth, caught perversely
wide, a universal fellatio, opened to make it look more
than shark enough; and even science will realise
that it's undead, its 'ka' and 'ba' fixed and lost
in equal measure, the flow of fluid not even providing
an optical illusion, no 'weighing of the heart'
beyond the heartlessness of curiosity.

Goat

Goat gone feral comes in where the fence is open
comes in and makes hay and nips the tree seedlings
and climbs the granite and bleats, through its line-
through-the-bubble-of-a-spirit-level eyes it tracks
our progress and bleats again. Its Boer heritage
is scripted in its brown head, floppy basset hound ears,
and wind-tunnelled horns, curved back for swiftness.
Boer goats merged prosaically into the feral population
to increase carcass quality. To make wild meat. Purity
cult of culling made vastly more profitable. It's a narrative.
Goat has one hoof missing—just a stump where it kicks
and scratches its chin, back left leg hobbling, counter-
balanced on rocks. Clots of hair hang like extra legs
off its flanks. It is beast to those who'd make devil
out of it, conjure it as Pan in the frolicking growth
of the rural, an easer of their psyches when drink
and blood flow in their mouths. To us, it is *Goat*
who deserves to live and its 'wanton destruction'
the ranger cites as reason for shooting on sight
looks laughable as new houses go up, as dozers
push through the bush, as goats in their pens
bred for fibre and milk and meat nibble forage
down to the roots. Goat can live and we *don't know*
its whereabouts. It can live outside nationalist tropes.
Its hobble is powerful as it mounts the outcrop
and peers down the hill. Pathetic not to know
that it thinks as hard as we do, that it can loathe
and empathise. Goat tells me so. I am being literal.
It speaks to me and I am learning to hear it speak.
It knows where to find water when there's no water
to be found—it has learnt to read the land
in its own lifetime and will breed and pass its learning
on and on if it can. Goat comes down and watches
us over its shoulder, shits on the wall of the rainwater
      tank—our lifeline—and hobbles off
        to where it prays, where it makes art.

Eagle Affirmation

You've got to understand that sighting the pair
of eagles over the block, right over our house,
not more than twenty feet above the roof,
so massive their wings pull at the corrugated
tin sheeting even with gentlest tilt, counteracts
bitterness against all the damage I see and hear
around me on an exclusively crisp blue morning,
when clarity is pain and even one small missing
wattle tree, entirely vanquished since I was last here
at home—I still find this hard to say—is agony;
a region is not a pinpoint and a different compass
works in my head, having magnetics for all
directions and all pointing to one spot
I know and observe as closely as possible;
and even one small vanished or vanquished
wattle tree is agony close to death for me,
where I find it hard to breathe to feed myself
to get past the loss; but the pair of eagles
still appearing and keeping their sharp
and scrupulous eyes honed, overrides
this ordeal, though I wish their victims
life too and their damage is traumatic
as anything else; that's as much sense
or nonsense as I can make in such blue light.

Sacred Kingfisher and Trough Filled with Water Pumped from Deep Underground

'[The written word] is the work of art nearest to life itself.'
—Thoreau ('Reading')

With the record heat I filled one of the three
concrete troughs—mainly for kangaroos
but also for birds and anything else that passes
by. This morning I saw a sacred kingfisher
in an overhanging branch, eyeing the water.
The sacred kingfisher saw me and remained.
That's unusual—they are mostly cautious.
I over-invest the 'sacred' in their name—name
giving, name evoking statistics from those
who've probably not even seen the bird. A small
bird with a large beak that could inflict a lot
of damage on whatever it targets. Proportional
and relative. Its colours are flashy and stunning.
What part do I play in filling the trough, once
for sheep and horses? How much choice
to come and go does the sacred kingfisher
have? Would it be here if the trough was empty?
The valley was quiet in the broadest sense.
I did not know how much noise was within
the bird's head. I thought of Thoreau
thinking of Alexander the Great carrying
the *Iliad* in a special casket. Which now
makes me think of a coffin. Water troughs
look like coffins, like caskets. I expected
the sacred kingfisher to swoop as if the shallow
water held nourishment. It was dead water
from deep in the earth. The sacred kingfisher
stayed in the branch, seeing the trough
for the coffin it was. The bird looked at me
then looked back to the lifeless surface
of the water. Still . . . so still.

Kangaroos in torchlight

Stillness makes you shiver inside, skin
unmoving; there is no part of our biographies
feeding the torchlight, only the kangaroos
trying to look gently past the flickering beam
at what's moving, what makes light out

of darkness; they don't get to select
their deaths and call it 'madness' or 'okay,
I took the risk', they just try
to stay out of its reach. In this
is the only immense spirituality

I believe, walking the long road
up the hill to close the gate, to close
in and protect what I'd like to think *they*
pass over, like our oversubscription
to the soul's persistence, or that some

memory will stick to rocks and soil,
stay close and bear light that seals
a nightworld in place, that we might absolve
the shaky clinginess of gravity: rather, all
imagined is partial indifference

of kangaroos by torchlight, stilled
to graze the dead grass of Elysian Fields
where nothing can die again, and few
will head back to that overwhelming light
that weighs so heavily on the living.

Balloon

It didn't happen in that order—
the endless growl of what will turn out to be
miniature quad and trailbikes, carried along
the top of the valley and rumbling its contents:
small kids with helmets weighing more than their heads,
ragged on by parents with crossed arms and ambition
in their eyes: round and round the drone of fun.
A country pursuit. Tracy tells me a professor
of economics at a local city university
while praising capitalism says he will only
listen to opposition if it comes from one
who eats only lentils, has given up cars
and eschews imported brands of foodstuffs. Lentils?
Contradictions aside, I'll take him on, though
it might be hard to hear me speak above the junior
quad-bike circus performing along the hills. But hark,
I'll tell you something unusually usual: at dusk
wandering the block with Katherine we came across
shreds of chemical-pink balloon with plastic string
attached to its tied-off umbilical cord, clearly
an escapee from a party, the child—her name
decorating the balloon with three crosses for kisses—
in tears, chasing it up into the sky, watching
it drift over the hills, her letter to the world
a single word and her mark made over. Katherine
asks if I recall the balloons her class back in England
released with school name and address and how one
floated all the way over the Channel and on to Belgium
where another child picked up the shreds and deciphered
the message and wrote back; weather balloons, 'hopes
and ambitions' as Delmore says, but without doubt
or scepticism, in full expectation they will land
somewhere far away and bring joy to the finder.
I dispose of the shred of balloon, fearing
an animal crossing the block in the dark,

night-eyed and keenly sampling the ground
and the air with its snout, will reread or misread
the code of chemical pinkness, and like some Red
Riding Hood in reverse, choke on the gift of chance.

from Réunion!

TROPICBIRDS

Here, on the island, it's the white-tailed
tropicbird, the *paille-en-queue*, with its straw
tail tillering updrafts of ravines, or pivoting
volcanic rock-faces. It resonates. But on a tiny,
flat atoll in the same ocean, I once saw red-tailed
tropicbirds, signature tails cutting sunsets,
papercuts in heavy clouds, the criss-cross
of bloodshot eyes. I am told they're here also—
nesting at the far reach of their domain—
but I doubt they'll show themselves. No flash.
No epiphanies. No past as bright as your future,
a redlining. But the white tails I see everywhere:
the slash where stone rises hot into colder air.
I lose the tone of whiteness to sunlight, and follow
its arrow west, witnessing its own will and testament,
quill to sign off and to affirm islands large
or infinitesimally small, maybe going under;
their ocean-tide's climb and descent.

BATS AT GRAND FOND

Tide swallows beach and even gentle breakers
push through from the reef over the lagoon
and darken the shore. The sun has left its cloud
and collapsed into a ruddy mess below the horizon.
We walk up the sandy passageway onto Avenue
Leconte de Lisle, and the pings of sonar catch
us at sharp angles, placing us in the depths
of Grand Fond, wings clicking to maintain
an illusion of invincibility; hunting mechanism.
Tim's first sighting of a bat. And there's no mistake.
The one signals many, a cloud outside meteorology—
storm warning or aftermath; a weather known to locals—

calling us out, to stand transfixed but insist that we
should move on, adjust our spiritual gain.

Ghostly as the claws of quick crabs on coral sand.
Evasive as *cabots sauteurs* on black volcanic rock.
Rectilinear as wooden pallets tossed-up on steep
beaches where no reef protects from the deeps.
Molosse bat? What *we* call 'freetailed bats'?
Likely, but there are also *Taphiens de Maurice*
and a cemetery by the sea, where prophets
and homeless men sleep by tombs. We stare
out to Madagascar and Africa, through wavering
skies. Maybe these *are* Mauritian Tomb Bats?
We hurry home. Did you see any white
on their chests, I ask? I don't think so, Tim says,
but it was hard to tell as the last light went fast.

LOOKING ACROSS LA PLAINE DES PALMISTES TO LE PITON DES NEIGES

Clouds fall away and the pastures hold lost forests.
The air clears and the cool settles to highlight
the 'dead' volcanic peak: key to this *young,*
growing island. We are outside The Flying Saucer—
Desperado Discothèque—'Soucoupe Volante'—
where an alien encounter bound the heritages
of islanders together—'African', 'Tamil', 'Chinese', 'French'—
the long lost palms—or is that giving too much
emphasis to what is the most popular and notorious
and probably isolated nightclub on the island?
Where vertigo is a painting never quite dry,
and ferns are inhabitants silently saying too much.

Sack

Ancient riverbed hacked and carved whittled deep
by winter run-off river as sudden as a dust storm
in the long summer red bed red dust caves haunting
level best upper storeys where sea breeze ratchets
off ocean and estuary black bream spiky and petrifying
in their pools cut-off omphaloi each and every one
an oracle of seams and joins worked by heat rising
and stretching to breaking point the ripple and crackle
of segregation; onto the sandy riverbed soft and cool
to feet when waded through like frothy low-level surf,
encapsulated by shadows crosshatching from river
red gums in nooks and crannies down down
from ledge, onto sand the flung sack came down on,
its pulsating and cavorting arc, aerodynamic mischief,
anomaly in flight to parabola and plunge to thud
and be absorbed into white sand reddening as hessian
soaks up last breaths and catfights and mews into grey
currawong and red-tailed black cockatoo distraction
and camouflage, seed-eaters and carnivores mixed
to a pitch of blur. And witnessed by teenagers mucking
about after school: sack wrenched straight from car
lurching on dirt track a lover's leap moth-eaten or chewed
to disappointment, the sack hurled up and down down
with such force the face of perpetrator lost or encrypted,
the type and colour of car forgotten, number plate
unthought of; just the sack now twitching between pools
shallowing with heat and red motes and litotes in the air,
choking and irritating, down down onto the cool sand
(sandals kicked off), to cut open the stitched-up sack
with a pocket knife and reveal the mince of kittens
all trauma and extinction and two or three
with mouths carelessly wired together, half-open
half-closed so their noises would come out all wrong.

The Fable of the Great Sow

Great Sow, who squashed dead her litter
A year before, rubbed her thick sparsely-haired
Hide pinker than pink against sty walls.
Flies and pig smells wrought hot under
Tin roof, wagtails working their way
Between pigs and dust and shit, picking off.
To cut across her pen was an act of dexterity.
A leap across the gate, a pivot on the wall
Opposite, and over into a neighbouring pen.
Short cut. I could have gone around. But
I'd done it before, and she looked so distractedly
Blissed in her deep scratch that I took the plunge.
Many times my weight, and half my
Stretch again in length. Reacted quick
And cut me off. Back then it would have
Been easy to talk of her malevolent eyes,
Her snotty nose, her deadly teeth.
Of all human warp embodied.
My wits were dulled. She was total pig,
Pure sow who'd farrowed litter on litter
To watch them raised to slaughter.
Fed on meal and offal, she'd been penned
With boars merciless in their concupiscence.
She had a reputation for violence against humans:
She loathed them. Us. Thirty years later,
I see James Ward's painting, *Pigs*, in the Fitzwilliam.
That shocks me into recollection. Grossed out,
Exhausted Sow, eye to the light made night
With a forward ear, milk-drained, piglets
Piled sleeping by her side, eternally confident,
Her Self replete in their growing natures.
Even the runt snuggles content in straw
As there'll be plenty in her sow abundance.
She has manufactured. And as Great Sow
Is about to charge and crush and tear
My childhood out of me, I take this picture
From my future, a painting from 1793,

A painting from nine thousand miles away,
Maybe in a place where Great Sow's ancestors
Planned their vengeance, passive for the artist,
Brewing generations of contempt inside.
A point of singularity is reached, epiphany
In straw and swill-filled air between us
(Normally, I would gate her out to change straw
And water). We both grunted and she went
Back to her scratching. I scurried out, neither
Runt nor star of her litter, her old fury lost
To pig history, flies and heat of the shed.

Sleeping with a Southern Carpet Python

Driving south to stay with my brother in the house
on the edge of great Dryandra Forest, refuge
of the stripy termite-eating numbat, I grind the gravel
across the one-lane bridge with its brief bitumen
respite, working strobe-lit shadows and corrugations,
keeping the vehicle centred. I am a young, embittered
father moving away from family ensconced in a low
and swampy suburb, a reclaimed rubbish tip at the base
of the Scarp. Now, eucalypts and parrots cluster
at the roadside, sheep working gnomic lines to dams,
the tinge of green of the new growing year, rancour
of salt scalds—I convince myself all call me home.
I grow steadily distracted with the brute subtleties
of dragging the back end of the car into shape,
a soft spot in the gravel pulling away from direction,
gyroscopic interlude. And then, before me *within*
braking distance, within the realm of breaking thought
to control the slide without three-sixtying into oblivion,
is an eight-foot southern carpet python at full stretch,
slowly negotiating the road, its cryptic rippling
a camouflage separated from its realm but working
black and gentle yellow-olive into the orange of gravel,
willing the gap to close, openness a trauma to be filed
under 'instinctual', an inverse constriction of mind
over matter. I skid right over it, crushing its tubular
body. I handle snakes. I have handled snakes since
the time I was warned not to go near, not to *touch*.
Deadly dugites and mulga snakes by the tail
or behind the head. To carry to safety, lift from roads
where they are . . . crushed. And this great snake,
distressed and writhing, python in need of a meal,
winter shutdown fast approaching, I lift and place
in folds of a tartan blanket on the back seat. Compacted,
splayed, its body hasn't burst: its hunger a blessing.
I drive to my brother's, where I place it deep down
within my sleeping bag. Warmth. (I still drank back then.
Heavily. And to oblivion.) When sleep drags me

to my sleeping bag, I don't think twice about crawling
in with the crippled, dying python. My life is lived
with sleep in glimpses, moments of nodding off,
so any sleep that comes is sleep I embrace—a sleep
with snakes is not a temptation, nor a loss. Insomniac,
I sleep deeply and in a dreamless stupor, though it has
since fed my nights with images and dark rumours.
Living dead, I still make body-warmth and the cold
blood of the snake exchanges its knowledge,
its stock of stories and experiences. When I wake
with the morning streaming coldlight into the room,
I shudder with poikilothermic thirst, clutching
the walls of my cocoon close, synapses tuning
to the expectation of snake at my feet, retracting
my toes and huddling to a ball. Emptiness.
I reach for my glasses and focus. The southern
carpet python, carpet snake of my childhood
I saw often on the farm coiled around log rafters
in the hay barn, rat-hunter and friend of the farmer,
warder-off of ill charms of presence, is sliding
alongside the walls, rounding the square room,
full of my body-warmth and raring to go.

Penillion for Pussy Riot

Faux fathers take
Pride away, rake
In the money
Quick fast and pray

Dead souls to make
The count, forsake
Their liberty.
'Security'

Is the serfdom
Of the kingdom
On earth: weapons-
Grade big truncheon

Penetration
To boost nation
Of God Father
To spite Mother.

Shake, rattle, roll.
Kiss sacred scroll
As if worship
Is the fillip

To topple self-
Styled god Himself,
Master icon
And his henchmen.

This is no stockade

This is no stockade
to keep them out;
this is no stockade
to take the brunt;
this is no stockade
to hold its own;
this is no stockade
to flag its moment.
This is no stockade
to vanguard a mine;
this is no stockade
to placate the boss.
This is no stockade
to count our loss;
this is no stockade
to surround or rally 'round;
this is no stockade
to watch over frontiers;
this is no stockade
to make last stands;
this is no stockade
to retreat into;
this is no stockade
from which to sally forth.
This is no stockade
of ordnance or survey;
this is no stockade
to store your relics.

Bushfire Approaching

I

I am ready to evacuate if need be.
My wife emailed to say a fire is out of control
on Julimar Road, less than ten kilometres away.
She says she'll return with the car, but I say it's okay,
we'll monitor and speak through the gaps.
She insists she will return: listening to the chat
in the library at Toodyay, seeing smoke in the west,
checking the FESA site. I say I will take a look outside
and get back to her in minutes. She is waiting. I climb
the block gingerly with my torn calf muscle striking back,
and see the growing pall over Julimar. A great firebreak
and a bitumen road are between here and there, I reassure,
though I will keep a close eye on it. The breeze blows
from the east, but is ambivalent and could swing
about. There are no semantics in this. And Paul Auster
is right where William (the lumberman) Bronk was wrong:
the poem doesn't happen in words, but 'between seeing
the thing and making it into a word'. *Location location location.*
As evidence: if fire sweeps through, only the mangled
metal of this Hermes typewriter will remain,
a witness, philosophy in-situ vanquished, and an elegy
made from bits of a different seeing with different words,
remain. Figurative density will take hold, and landscape
will be less fragile, the font more robust. It won't rely
on paper: ash become an idea, a taste for some.
You stop seeing the red when it's on top of you.
But true burning feeds on ash and the idea
of fire: it perseveres and requires only oxygen
and memory. Wild oats caught in my socks
taunt my ankles. Fuel for fire. In all seriousness.

II

I am not hearing AC/DC's 'This House Is on Fire'
out of perversity. This morning a rush of colour
brought on a flashback, and I've not had one of those
for a decade. Strychnine-saturated, like the bush
where rangers claim to conserve native species
through poisoned baits. Rapid heartbeat, dry mouth,
outbreaks of laughter (grotesque, face of death),
colour codings of annihilation: spiritual and topographical.
Phantasm of acid trips—pink batts, supermen, green dragons,
orange barrels, purple hearts, clearlights, ceramic squares,
goldflakes, microdots, lightning bolts: nomenclature
of William Blake and weird melancholy of habitat loss.
Lost and unfounded. A run on images. Voices in the room.
Excruciating paranoid cartoon violence. So, I check
outside again and the plume is still moving southwest
though the wind is tentative and temperature
up five degrees over the last thirty minutes. This is realtime,
unlike hypnagogia, hallucinations? Grounds for worship.
Foundational ontology. I should mention that I have flu
and that's why I stayed home in the first place. Harvest
is full-on though I have finished grass cutting here.
I wore myself out and my defences are down. Run down.
Antibodies hesitant if not docile. I make rhetoric
out of the flood of image-fragments: seems like good sense,
making the best, keeping a grip, cool in a volatile situation?

III

I'm abandoning my poem on the wheatbelt stone gecko
and the 'keeled tail' of a black-headed monitor
which is running amok through the roof, along walls,
scaling trees with maritime skill. The images lack
explanation and coalesce, are minimalist, but will
serve as a poor kind of last will and testament.
One sheet in my pocket, and it will be this.

IV

The wind has dropped, though smoke—not impenetrable
but more substantial than 'thin'—hangs over the block,
a tentative fallout. The birds are doing their silence
thing, or have shot through. We keep no birds in coops.
The air is almost acrid. Defend or abandon?
It's when the smell of burning reaches upwind
that you know it has bitten deep. Firebreaks: check.
Water: check, but if the pump goes that's an end to flow.
Fireblanket: check. Personal papers and evacuation pack: check.
No room for 'literature': just this poem, paperweight.
Ready to lend a helping hand: always, to best of ability.
Essential medications. Maybe the boy's most precious toy,
but he wouldn't expect it. Something of my wife's.
Insects thick on the flyscreens: suddenly Hitchcockian.

V

Smoke-mushrooms are haloes about wattles they haven't yet touched
where it counts. Prelude. Early life of devastation, its long legacy
too long in its brief moment of, well, beauty. Back again after
staggering uphill—glimpses of lush green moss amidst stubble
and granite are bemusing and bizarrely cheering—and all is suddenly
military, war zone, combat. Helitacks, fixed-winged water bombers
coming over the hills. Dousing. Or maybe it's anti-militaristic?
No time to think about this. Three years ago, fire destroyed
forty homes just south of here. It was like this then, too.

VI

Alert Level: 'a bushfire is burning near Julimar and Kane Roads';
'stay alert and monitor your surroundings'; why use quote marks?
This is barely copyright in the life and death of it. Plagiarism?
Blame burns with a heat unlike any other and burns long
after last embers have faded. And with days of heat and high
winds ahead, even a dead ember might find heart again, and leap
to the occasion. Elemental showdown. Proof. Precedent.
Test case. Habeas corpus—the body present. The burning
question: people build houses in the bush, then blame the bush.
My brother, life-long surfer, says: If I get taken by a shark
remember it was while doing something I love in *its* universe.
Remember me in this light. The fire has jumped Julimar Road.

Freeing a Mouse from the Humane Trap Around Midnight

Towards midnight, I set out across the block
with a mouse in the 'humane trap': to release
into a moonless dark, up near the western fence,
among granites and fallen trees, dry and whittled-
back by the sun, wind, and entropy: refuges
for the little grey tremblers transferred from the house
in this time of 'mouse plague'—an abundance
of mice in roof and walls, running the frame,
reminding me of childhood and the farm
when panels in outbuildings collapsed
under the weight of field-mice boiling over,
or when lifting a sheet of corrugated iron
from the ground sent grey sparks flying
in all directions after strange attractors:
not chaos, but a perfect illustration
of transitivity, rapid dispersal with micro-
decisions made according to threat
and geography, what was known and what
was aberrant. So, walking the stony hillside,
torchlight wavering in one hand, trap in the other,
a strong wind dulling the senses, threatening
to bring down overhanging branches,
a vertigo of expectation: the predictable
(a route in daylight I have walked so often)
with the unknown, what darkness throws
to change the course of a life, my life, the mouse's.
So, walking the stony hillside, I operate within
safety limits, can tread with reasonable doubt
while being cautious, but approaching
the wire fence into the reserve, anxiety
and vertigo increase and a strange test-
case is pushed to the extreme. I tell myself
that this has nothing to do with 'property',
but everything to do with boundaries.
That's what's familiar and why it's familiar.
So, walking the stony hillside, I grow more
disorientated. Sensing the boundary,

I free the mouse. I understand its attempts
to hop back into the trap before embracing
torchlight and staring me down, turning tail
and racing towards the wire, the pitch-black.

Native Cutwood Deflects Colonial Hunger

Why 'raspberry jam tree'? *Acacia acuminata*. Mungart.
The guilt of cutwood? Its smell, its bloody show?
And that colourist's jam envy, the lust for ropes
of raspberry. Fence-posts sturdy and hardy
and doused in creosote: to stand alone
in termitesville. The sweetness turns rust.
And burnt offerings unless dried right through—
say for a year on the pile. Hot as hell to fire.
Nothing comes cost-free, we hear—those layers
of its dozen years a demonstration in history
as accumulation. Collective survey of occupation:
the real *corps de ballet*, the shrubby scenery,
bulldozed on roadsides. Ring-a-ring-a-rosy.
All those brandings. Emblem of *our town*
that would miss no more than our rates.
'High turnover' region. Think raspberry
jam on white damper, think coals of fires.
The meagre shade for sheep and cattle
and the denial of 'unproductive' animals.
Nuisances. Saw deep into rough bark,
showered in pollen. Unholy fires
at the end of winter; and all that premonition,
all those seeds with snow in their bellies,
snow that can't fall from this faraway sky.
So overwhelmingly familiar to me.
No Old Country raspberry homesickness.
Just an inkling of anthocyanin pigments.
Why 'raspberry jam tree'? *Acacia acuminata*. Mungart.

Comatos and Lacon

How likely is it that the fellas who have
moved onto a place down the loop, who
are bricking their crossover, are named
Comatos and Lacon? That they have
brought a small herd of goats with them,
and play guitars outside their house-shed
as the summer sun is setting purple on the hills?
If I say, It's entirely true! will you believe
that they are more than mythology,
that the sweat they drop onto the hillside
will erupt into an army of teeth-gnashers,
that they will join ranks and roll into
the brook and down into the river
and on to the sea? That oceans will rise
because of them? And what if I add,
It's in your best interest to believe
because this is the only reality left
to us, that even up here with great
plains spreading below us, oceans
of tears will soon be lapping at our feet,
and the goats will bleat their warning.

When a Big Animal Dies

When a big animal dies
it's so confronting the proportions
of life alter—all those small deaths
are magnified to their real size
& shockwaves drive final breaths—

the offbeat lift & fall
of a cow's flank, struck & *struck*
again on the asphalt altar, shadow
spread over lane with a sliver
of moon overhead, barely

a crescent in its great eye.
When a big animal dies
in your life, in front of you,
in medias res, you watch
on in horror, helpless

as you too have come close
to last breaths, with only a late swerve,
a gashing side-swipe, keeping
time & space in synch,
a possible onward journey

sketched out, not in the cloud
of breath rising into darkness,
escaping. How did you stray
into such a fate, cowlife
bred for death & this death

outside the scheme? What
holy nights are made from circles
of fire eating circles—stubble
burn that engulfs bushland, smoke
choking up what's left

to gift a barely
expanding universe?
All of this on one night,
one occasion, one encounter—
when a big animal dies.

Frankenthaler Paintings

Mountains and sea are a long way from here.
One mountain is within driving range,
but the nearest chain is far south and eroded.
We are on the edge of hills, shoulder
of a range that reaches down to the plains.
Sea is a flavour of breeze or the kick
of a winter storm fed by valleys
far away. Colour seeps back and forth:
'landscape in my arms as I did it':
mottles up awash to particularise
                    circuit of states: gaseous act of seeing,
fluid exhibition, inhabitation of what's gone back over

remember seeing: colour is fingerprint
                    greenly piquant (leaf litter)
          archaic uses of egregious
sets the polluted river on its estuarial watch
to suit development collocations (yes, 'heinous crime' IS
apt)
          all that's left intact is the act
of seeing, splashing in the rock, climbing faces
of waves;

                    but sea wrestles with horizontals, a curve
complex, calenture betrayed by swell
and dead coral underpinnings:
                              'mass,' says the critic
'eats at edges of heartland, as patriotic subterfuge';

consequent sails plume to claim the resistant
to occupy in studio aftermath
                              concomitant to gnash
against the rocks and wash up wheatbeach

burials: shared history, shared gestations
of charrings.

MAUVE DISTRICT (FRANKENTHALER, 1966): 2012

Sunset and this is it. This is that.
I'd fill it with Nude, but it doesn't
look the part. Nude is more or less,
and moves differently. Each her own.
Each face each sun each opacity on the window.
It's a precise map here where maps are doubtful.

I'd swear more it's the southwest shape
I'd swear the shape midpoint of hillside
looking out I'd swear the mauve is shape
I am inside looking out into, I'd swear.

Yes, yes, edges and light here, too.
But no luck in the degraded off-green
which hangs in there: scraped, dug, weeded
out to meet shire quotas to fuel unloading
continuous occupation in bundles of lingering
daylight to placate night's desire for absolution.

I left off this image because the light wasn't right:
not nearly mauve enough which bespoke qualities
elicited from even thin-lensed eyesight searching
for colour to sign off, relocate certainty in shadow
or trees obscuring starlight, but less than warmth
was never mauve enough: Now, it is right. Now!

I'd swear more it's the southwest shape
sold as visit to this state of solid light,
place of transition and leisure where locals
wear costs without complaint: dipping with sunlight.

CATERPILLAR TIME
and (partially) thinking of Frankenthaler's Yellow Caterpillar *(1961)*

One sections its way along the wall at right angles to round
the square off, hypotenuse its convertible self.
Bursting with transformative zeal and information, it homes
in on a place of purchase.

Shuffle leg diorama shunting appendages on scruffy bark
to reach lush leaf fans.

Yellow interior is not digestive hoodwink but internal aura
I can only guess at—all external beauty, holy inside & out.

Head reaching up to blue slab of sky and knitting vista
with immaculate movements of mouth,

never allow accidents when they cross the paths: never never never:
keep an eye out as they do, close to it all. Real close.

Soft sparks to jump gaps everywhere out there: or suckering
up the window to reveal the belly of the future.

We are talking about *art* here. Just because I look out into
a caterpillar world of Latin names and their backwash . . .

Between stages maybe, but such glorious intactness and self-
sufficiency. Glory glory glory.

Conversions of moisture and dryness, solidity and fluidity
in the crossing and dwelling. The hairiness.

Dark markers of digested presence to give back and sign,
never retaliate though some parody the fierce.

At the precise point of day when last rites are taken: the day
predator birds last gasp last swoop heat signature switching over

to nightbirds infrared standover tactics but to be pierced
to the vitals by the last swoop of day murdered

as dark falls, nightcap where weird isn't a word with grip
as the gatekeepers condemn analogies.

HINT FROM FRANKENTHALER
(after Hint from Bassano, *1973)*

Craven as flight, unremitting
as eye clashing with ear,
stumbling towards Egypt,
the entire family loaded
with an angel winging
a path of light: discordant
and smooth, precise as wind
rippling over grass (inside of a wave)
outside your window as if beauty is in every
grain of sand lodging in cracks,
gritting up the works.

When green and blue are no longer here, exile is beyond redemption.
Angles of disquietude containing smudge of lifespan and mechanism
of movement, tamas and hope as burning aftermath: chill effect
in the heat, land's backwash an injection of your own blood
into the failure of colour, labile saturate loss, though impelled
forward as back isn't an option and sideways disperses manifests
and records journeys, how much is in the stroke of chronicle,
or wing strokes and the uplift playing off the muted downforce.

Degeneracy of green, spread
sheet to catch fallout, driven

servitude and mastery, granaries
of GM corn enveloped from imposed
rat tumours, exceeding the 90 days
test limit though still denied
by the village's scribes and despots
and their patrician rushes of blood.

'Mouths all coloured green'

'No spectacle was more frequent in the ditches of towns, and especially in wasted
counties, than to see multitudes of these poor people dead with their mouths all
coloured green by eating nettles, docks, and all things they could rend above ground.'
—Fynes Moryson in 1601

When we were broke
and living 'down South'
in the shack, we boiled
and ate nettles and dock.

Our watertank poisoned
and the greens tainted,
we grew sicker by the day.
The 'boys' wanted us out

of the district, our mouths
'coloured green'. The English
starved the Irish on the order
of the Queen, ditches full

of the green-mouthed dead,
surfeited on 'all things they
could rend'. A template for
the Great Chain of Being.

Above board, below ground.
The 'boys' and their families
defended Queen and Country,
joined the military. Grotesque

is a quality of patterns
and not an act of decoration.
Is it improper of me to suggest
correlations—my ancestors
        famine migrants?

Hiss

At Lough Hyne parents rouse kids
to hiss but condemn the hissy-fit
when the order to cease
is ignored, all incited and in the grip.

Over-leaning a stone wall, stirring
a pair of mute swans to eloquence,
the combined hisses
trigger a localised squall—

an infectious hyperactivity
that makes an outing in 'nature'
an addictive spree, a confrontation
with beauty incarnate: the swans

disdainful of such mockery,
glaring back down their beaks
at parents whose cygnets
are floundering in the deep.

Fingerprints Lacking in Bantry

To register a presence, the ancestral
fingerprint irrelevant to the Garda,
you place a finger on the glass
glowing red, blood offering,
and the officer says try again,
roll your finger, take some natural
oil from behind your ear and press
on the glass again, roll your finger.
And still no print will show.
Decades ago your prints were taken
in ink when there was still enough
of you to show, confirm
what they didn't want.
Have you worked with chemicals?
Laboured on a farm or in a factory?
That will do it, she says. I've seen
prints of a bookish man of seventy
that are so beautifully preserved
he could still be a child. But yours
aren't even a shadow of what you were,
burnt off and never coming back.
Great storms a fortnight ago
threw waves and seaweed
up into the Garda station,
picked away at the seawall.
The tidal surge that will
reach to the bay's elbow,
main town of the region.
Mountains hold it in place,
but denuded of their copper souls,
they too have lost their prints.
And the old forests have gone.
Little is left of the stretches of oaks.
And I have these blank fingers,
these shiny hands, made
of the emptying out, the tendency
to go elsewhere and wear

new worlds to the bone.
We'll deal with this situation
at the next stage, she says,
when residency wants
more than prints,
when you'll pay.

Otter & Seal
in Schull Harbour
for Tim, and for John Kerrigan

1.

Pier's end betokens
cored discs of fireworks,
distraught wrappers

of celebration, of spent
rapture through drizzle
which holds Clear Island;

a harbour seal bottles,
snorts air with traces of salt solution,
and, yes, *studies* us—off starboard

an otter lifts and rises
higher than any spring metal,
falls back to twist into drift

with compulsion; otter & seal
enact within recall of dazzle—
fireworks suppressed to memory,

filtered out into harbour,
glimmer off grey-green surface
without sun, a daytime

resuscitation of fishways,
small trawlers stilled to death
at their moorings, and landdogs

running to the pier
to pursue otter & seal
against medium, against restraint,
land to air to water.

2.

The story of seeing
should not be forgotten
by the teller—called out

to engage otter, called out
to engage seal, adding circles of witness,
gathering vision of seal *and* otter—

fraternal, paternal, fluid
as soup of harbour with dross
and essential ingredients,

the heavy hunting zone
no one's leisure, but all between
is essential also, matters more,
        submariners.

3.

I have been obsessed with otters
since reading *Ring of Bright Water*
as a seven-year-old near the otterless

river of my Australian childhood, where water
rats came up through torrefied gardens
and dropped dead on back lawns,

and where water rat vs. otter
matched creature with reading
rather than creature to speech.

Obsessed. Then I let go and let
water rat be water rat, and Scotland
be Scotland. And now

in this Ireland we construct
return on return that is nothing
and everything to do with a presence,

in zone of otter speech and seal reading,
of thought and utterance—*listen and hear*. . .
to the slip of water, the oil of fur

and breath overload with snort of seal.
Exhalation. Vapour. Together and not, they
work the waterishness, looking to blackened
red rock edge, where to emerge, consider.

4.

Water and fire: breakdown
of spectrum. So much of 'home' burns
and here it drizzles on and on in emergence,

the inflamed ambience of 'celebratory' afterthought:
residues, pollutants, discards, ingredients
of fireworks and bait, the schools of fish

a diver (compact bird?) goes for, too, small
and abrupt and glossed, rising from under.
Submergences and emergences, from slip to glide

to smoke, to drift, to drizzle, to slide to storm—
fireworks—oxidation counterpoint
as all air is sucked out from where
we come from—evacuating, now, GMT?

Borromini's Perspective and the Galleria Spada's Resident Cat

'The cat becomes a tiger in there, and the statue becomes so small.'
    —Valentina (at the front desk)

Seventy centimetres or thereabouts of Roman warrior
down the columns and arches to a vanishing point
all thirty-five metres we envisage as not much more
than eight, all those tricks of desire for more

than we can see, all those answers to immensity.
Green oranges brash as ripeness to come,
and bold cat full of God and Sun preening
a corner to soften the lines, make geometry

a choice, organically precise. I ask Valentina
if he wanders further than the chain which no
visitor can pass, and she ululates and insists
he becomes tiger while the statue diminishes—

that small warrior in all of us showing off,
law of the jungle, wildcat in its lair, focal point
of those empires we make from art, envisage
when enemy troops are at the city's gates.

The Bulldozer Poem

Bulldozers rend flesh. Bulldozers make devils
of good people. Bulldozers are compelled to do
as they are told. Bulldozers grimace when they

tear the earth's skin—from earth they came.
Bulldozers are made by people who *also* want new
mobile phones to play games on, *and* to feed families.

Bulldozers are observers of phenomena—decisions
are taken out of their hands. They are full of perceptions.
They will hear our pleas and struggle against their masters.

Bulldozers slice & dice, bulldozers tenderise, bulldozers
reshape the sandpit, make *grrrriiing* noises, kids' motorskills.
Bulldozers slice the snake in half so it chases its own tail,

writing in front of its face. Bulldozers are vigorous
percussionists, sounding the snap and boom of hollows
caving in, feathers of the cockatoos a whisper in the roar.

Bulldozers deny the existence of Aether, though they know
deep down in their pistons, deep in their levers, that all
is spheres and heavens and voices of ancestors worry

at their peace. Bulldozers recognise final causes, and embrace
outcomes that put them out of work. There's always more
scrub to delete, surely . . . surely? O *continuous tracked tractor,*

O *S* and *U* blades, each to his orders, his skillset. Communal
as D9 Dozers (whose buckets uplift to asteroids waiting
to be quarried). O bulldozer! your history! O those Holt tractors

working the paddocks, O the first slow tanks crushing
the battlefield. The interconnectedness of Being. Philosopher!
O your Makers—Cummings and Caterpillar—O great *Cat*

we grew up in their thrall whether we knew it or not—playing
sports where the woodlands grew, where you rode in after
the great trees had been removed. You innovate and flatten.

We must know your worldliness—working with companies
to make a world of endless horizons. It's a team effort, excoriating
an ecosystem. Not even you can tackle an old-growth tall tree alone.

But we know your power, your pedigree, your sheer bloody
mindedness. Sorry, forgive us, we should keep this civil, O dozer!
In you is a cosmology—we have yelled the names of bandicoots

and possums, of kangaroos and echidnas, of honeyeaters
and the day-sleeping tawny frogmouth you kill in its silence.
And now we stand before you, supplicant and yet resistant,

asking you to hear us over your war-cry, over your work
ethic being played for all it's worth. Hear us, hear *me*—
don't laugh at our bathos, take us seriously, forgive

our inarticulateness, our scrabbling for words as you crush
us, the world as we know it, the hands that fed you, that made you.
Listen not to those officials who have taken advantage

of their position, who have turned their offices to hate
the world and smile, kissing the tiny hands of babies
that you can barely hear as your engines roar with power.

But you don't see the exquisite colour of the world, bulldozer—
green is your irritant. We understand, bulldozer, we do—
it is fear that compels you, rippling through eternity,
        embracing the inorganics of modernity.

Milking the Tiger Snake

Fangs through a balloon, an orange balloon
stretched over a jam-jar mouth scrubbed-up
bush standard—fangs dripping what looks
like semen which is venom, one of the most
deadly, down grooves and *splish splash*
onto the lens of the distorting glass-bottom
boat we look up into, head of tiger
snake pressed flat with the bushman's
thumb—his scungy hat that *did Vietnam,*
a bandolier across his matted chest
chocked with cartridges—pistoleer
who takes out ferals with a secretive
patriotic agenda. And we kids watch
him draw the head of the fierce snake,
its black body striped yellow. 'It will rear
up like a cobra if cornered, and attack,
attack!' he stresses as another couple
of droplets form and plummet. And when
we say, 'Mum joked *leave them alone
and they'll go home,*' he retorts, 'Typical
bloody woman—first to moan if she's bit,
first to want a taste of the anti-venom
that comes of my rooting these black
bastards out, milking them dry—down
to the last drop.' Tiger snake's eyes
peer out crazily targeting the neck
of the old coot with his dirty mouth,
its nicotine garland. He from whom
we learn, who shows us porno
and tells us what's what. Or tiger snake
out of the wetlands, whip-cracked
by the whip of itself until its back is broke.

Emily Brontë Storm Poem

The storm isn't here.
It isn't predicted. And yet
the barometer's
needle has cast its lot—

down past the leaf, even,
down to the floor—
all is stagnant, *no*, a tremble of door
& window, ants moving in—

I am withdrawn & extrovert,
making sure things are
secure. Nature is life, & a bout
of high wind and sparks stirs

us to friction—what can
be destroyed needs following-
up with acts of conservation.
The storm is approaching—

no, it is always here,
building above & below us,
though skies remain clear.
No, the blue slightly feathers.

The White Rose: With a Glimmer of Blake's Illustration for Dante's *Paradise* Canto 31

'The two fountains were given to the university by the city in 1877 as a gift for its 400th birthday. The fountains were removed in 1931 in order to use the square in front of the assembly hall for National Socialist rallies. An artistic foundry in Süßen cast the fountains anew and in 1999 they were again installed in their original location, now called the Scholl-Sibling-Square, named after the famous siblings who were members of the White Rose resistance movement.'
—Universitätsstadt Tübingen*

The fountains are dry. But then late snow falls on them
and they briefly turn into white roses. Brother and sister fountains.
Resurrected. Students buzz around, checking their phones,

comparing marks, joking about *Ordnung* society
they will graduate into. I cut across the square twice
a day, but only today I see the fountains as the white roses

they are. A few weeks ago young people were handing
out leaflets. I did not take one. I do not know what they were
saying, what they were disseminating. I should have enquired.

The fountains look identical but are different. When they are
alive under sunshine people will remark on the prisms of light.
The Nazis cut out the fountains. They wanted room to move.

In each petal of the white rose hope arose. In the silent
early hours of morning, creatures move about here we don't
see in daylight, not even at night with its residues of wakefulness.

I was reminded of this today, chatting with a friend. Snow dissolving.
When I was a child, my cousins and I broke up sheets of asbestos
with our grandfather and jigsaw-puzzled it around his beds of roses.

* http://tuebingen-info.de/index.php?id=812&sav_library=908e661515b0012103672&cHash
=1196c4dbe1c4f58a92c12d8f0e37ef3d

Broke the sheets into fragments. Like smashing bottles
at the tip; it was great fun. The roses grew as well as ever,
and the asbestos rested under a tarp of gravel. Some were

white roses. The knowledge of the White Rose resistance,
its civil disobedience, its refusal of violence, gives me that hope.
Over seventy years later and I can see the faces of the Scholls

and their friends in the students handing out leaflets. I don't
know anything about these people, don't know where they were
born or where they come from or what their 'ethnicities' are.

I don't know what they are saying. But I see the faces
of the Scholls and their friends, I see the overlapping flesh
of the flower, so perfect it might sit in the sick rooms of those

suffering from mesothelioma. My grandfather loved roses.
He did not understand about asbestos. He was horrified by
the Nazis and all they did, thousands of miles away.

If I am here again when the fountains are full, I will stare
through the spray, through the rose of water into their calyces.
In the broken mirror I will search my face and ask of myself.

Denkmal: Tübingen

This won't be held by a template.
No Blake, no Dante, no Hölderlin
can grasp it. If I had Hebrew

I would write a sonnet. I would
take the few words of Hebrew Dante
uses and liberate them from

their model. Nothing can prepare
one for the impact of the site, a monument
to absence. An apartment sits

on the site at the Synagogenplatz,
just up from the hydroelectric plant
on the Neckar River, water falling

fast through, lower lower. And
thirty mute swans facing upstream,
still as the quiet expected

on a Sunday afternoon. When
Nazis came with their backers,
they burned the synagogue

from the flank of the Österberg,
a flurry of activity down the Gartenstrasse,
the Jewish community made to pay—

literally pay—for the destruction.
Some critics say Dante was *above*
the medieval Christian habit

of distorting Jews, of blaming
them for sins of a material world.
Absence speaks louder?

Reading the names of people
driven from their homes, or murdered
in the orderly buildings of the camps,

names cut into rusty metal plate,
the fountain dry with winter,
I collapse all history of the town

to this site. As creating the university
in the late fifteenth century, the founders
ensured Jews were driven away,

separating part of their own identity,
the answers to purpose and eternity.
And to repeat the crime. Red

as any tint in a Blake illustration.
Even the songbirds alighting
from the peak shimmer and blur

in the absorption. As after the war
retired Nazis favoured the monastic
village of Bebenhausen, god and the hunt,

great antlers on barns and over
front doors, bristling with their mix
of charm and luck and bloodlust.

And that was only last week.
This Denkmal, which so many
pass without registering.

The massacre sites of the world
are in constant communication:
the sparks that pass between

are the essences of all prayer
thrown about, all prayer left hanging
in the air waiting to collect somewhere.

To pray without naming death?

Bat! in Tübingen, Late Winter

I have been watching a bat working the inside
of a right-angled triangle of buildings just outside
this window. Dusk is slow coming on and the bat
is sharp and slow-quick and induces a compulsion
to mimic. I read that no bats ever really get entangled
in hair, that this is pure folklore. But I have seen
it happen in childhood. Witness. The squeaking I hear
is really a chirp chirp bat hears and overhears
as it takes three storeys of the building I am
encased in, rides the insect columns up up
up then drops to skim over the top of the thin
and shallow but fast Ammer River. Skim is not
a truly accurate description of its movement
which is terse, jerky, but fluid. I am fixated.
Writing and watching at once. Caught up.
Entangled. This is no self-projection, and this
is no description. Snub-body is airborne
of exquisite ragged wings. I am not becoming bat
and I don't wish anything else on it. I am not
the bat on the stick from the showbag, one
of eight my father gave us each on an access
visit, an outing to the Royal Show, 1975. But
I loved that rubber bat, bouncing in front
of my mother, my brother. My father
never saw it. Bat is small by my measure
but a giant to insects, overwhelmed I must
state the obvious, reiterate. Precise and close
to the glass like ethics. The window
is partially open. It is winter. Late winter.
Bat is not from the cellar of the castle
but maybe from the patchy woods near-
by. Telephone repeaters work the invisible.
I am vulnerable to the signals, the crackle I think.
A slow-down, a flutter, my arrhythmia
to offset dying light. Mammalian flower,
take this down as a rant and ramble,
Hölderlin in Zimmer's tower,

making it his own, seasonal adjustment,
SAD, listen listen! Bat is not performing
as it's supposed to? It is at the glass.
It taps. I am not even suggesting a code.
They don't do that. They don't. Never never never!
Years and years in caves and I've never seen
it happen, says the researcher. Never ever ever!
Well, be here, be here, eye to eye, now. So close.
Body warmth. Cold hardening, viscous
to force on through. Wings mirroring
insects suddenly alight from within.

Sweeney the thesaurus bird

Sweeney the thesaurus bird doesn't want to be scribed
into any monk's poem. A telling of his doings—no, more

than this: it's as if they know him. So many spatial
and temporal issues it's not worth unfurling feathers.

The yellow or green belly of the ringneck parrot,
one or the other outside its range: him or another?

But he did alight as a pronoun on the whipping branches
of a jam tree that had been killed but still looked sprightly.

Death doesn't creep up; rather, life doesn't arrive
as it once did. The bark-strippers had been to the picnic

spots to strip from head to toe, the leaves laughing
nervously, affect inappropriate. He knows the killers

to be strung out, off their faces, hanging, ripped, blown
away, smashed, blotto, fucked-up, desperate. Greedy.

To take the bark and make a tea, distil it to the essence
of leaf-shaped clouds, green sky and blue ground. Trippy.

DMT—dimethyltryptamine—extracted from the hallowed
tree, short-lived tree revered for the flour its seeds provide.

The parrot's belly is an hallucination. There is no red ridge
over its beak. It's hard to pick whether it's male or female.

The picnic is defamiliarised and the words for replete
and lack are caught up in the brocade of antonyms

and synonyms. Who's watching the thieves? Dead
perches are disconnection from the earth which speaks

through a taut wire and two tin cans, vibrations
along the line. It's hard to weave a nest

when there are no eggs to be laid. He says this.
Or the druggies say it. It's on the breeze,

that's for sure—going nowhere,
out of whack with its fate.

Sweeney Inside the Wound, the Graveyard, the Deathzone

Accompanying the red-tailed black cockatoos,
Sweeney wavered in the brittle air and plummeted
deep into the wound, the graveyard, the deathzone.

Gasping, he knew immediately that he'd be violently ill,
that The One who had been going *to & fro, up & down*
across the damaged earth, would smite him also,

mark him with the indelible blood of the wound.
The mountain of uprooted grass trees, their name—*balga*—
resonating through future epochs of pitch and sulphur,

and marri trees that won't ever blossom again,
the torn capillaries and veins of time, all wondering
if they be dead or undead, sap retreating with syntax,

photosynthesis in slow shutdown. Sweeney spoke
loud to the man-becoming-cockatoo—James—to whom
the policeman had said, 'Get away or I will kneecap you',

who beheld the betrayers and documented The Fall—
cockatoo with clipped wings, disorientated inside
the wound the graveyard the deathzone.

After Hölderlin's 'Friedensfeier'

It's out of my hands, but here is a sample. All those words dressed up as song filling my ears from the denuded fringes of city.

A woodchipper is eating the cut branches
and cut trunks of trees deemed unnecessary—
it's been going on for weeks—and the grinding-
chewing effect is an affect without a single note
of sweetness, and now a chainsaw—no getting
away from them in any of the treed places
of the world, and the hills cushion the hacking
reverberation, force it through their syrinxes.
It's all collusion from municipal elsewheres,
from civic buildings in the old town,
the zigzag of ancient wood mimicry,
as nightfall approaches and those
last organics are spat into the receptacle.

But I have my eyes and ears peeled,
listening beyond the deathsounds, waiting
to catch the late-early calls of the riverbird.
It sticks around through winter, making
the best of what's on offer. Generations
of conflict along these narrow banks,
the poisoned grasses, the long-gone
common reeds. But I am standing
in for you in this celebration of peace
talks—the connivings of Munich
to let death stop in Syria, a bit.
God has decided on unity.
A shell burst antiphony.

But I am not the protagonist of this text.
That is you. And when I say I, I mean you.
It's about the space we occupy and what is claimed.
How much is apportioned to the bargaining table.
Which fragment of us will fit where. Oriental.

Occidental. What is a 'country' where well over
ten percent of the population has been eliminated?
Strain to hear the glorious Muwashshah through the AK47
death rattle, the artillery barrages. Which feast day
are we celebrating? What dangles from the gunbelt?
What corruption of the sacral, of the rhyme
that plays on eternity, the irrelevance of time,
the beat of the darabukkah embracing the sublime
strains of oud and qanun. What of these flowers
in the spiritual garden, the banquet hall
of old men and old women and the young
who accompany them? What of them all? What of Aleppo?

We would invite you over but the water
is so deep, is so wide, is so measured by the weight
of coin fallen through its bloody nets over millennia.
That Syrian palm. Elusive shade. The testy winter sun.
As the monuments fall to the bloody-minded, the clouds
refuse to carry you anywhere. Flight. And now to 'fight
people smugglers' you have your NATO warcrafters
patrolling to benefit us all. In the wild places
of European cities, where the balance of nature
is so delicate. Deadly as the shadows of houses on houses,
on the historic tourist places we celebrate. Heaven
sends its boats. You can all be on them.

All this fire. Bricks and mortar and metal
and flesh burn easily. These otherworld attacks,
right out from the rim of a Philip K. Dick replica
solar system. Those lively banters in the drone
HQ. Smart phones that find their way
into any wartorn store. Effective distribution.
Demand supply is demanded. A music of joyousness,
the timbre of the praying human voice.
It chooses to pray. It is not compelled.
To drift over the ocean floor,
to bob in the waves, to driftwood

the beaches. Remember, 'movement
of the people'! We have forgotten about
them all, and forget ourselves as we move
further in. Or fly over, wanting the kinder sun.

So we're asked to stop what we're doing
and do it another way. Who is doing the asking?
Silence works the conventions of language. It's a mask.
Each word added to the lexicon, dragged
into the pop-cultural whirlpool. Where can we hide
in the sensorium? We find ourselves out, the multiplication
of images weighing down the memory banks of world.
Red kite, barbary falcon, Syrian ostrich, little grebe, pharaoh eagle-owl; goldcrest.
From this point to that. All the way up to the levelling-off.

   Don't underestimate the amount of time spent
wondering how much of creation a single *Hypecoum grandiflorum* (Papaveraceae)
occupies. The contemplation that has no news conference, that will not
prove Einstein right (always right), that will not challenge the gasp
of a black hole, the weight of the sun that draws it out of itself,
makes grow. In the stench of body decay, the stench
of explosives, the stench of testosterone mirroring megalomania,
the human condition mutates. Even on feast-days, someone
is out of kilter, someone is on a different timetable.
Bomb first, party later. And so held is all dominion.
This proof sheet. Negative when negatives
aren't to be found blown hot in the rubble, washed in the sea. Old ways.

   Hymns and thunderstorms. Cloud-seeding.
Autobiographies of weather. Borders selectively porous.
We the blessed, we the cherished, we the children of,
stunted. Gather the flock. Wash the feet.
Eat delicacies after the hot sun has set,
a dusting of snow not far south of Munich.
And mountains, ominous mountains, nearby.
And so immortality is handed out,
doled out, ladled and deposited and secured.

The house is open the house is full
the house is bombed by those who made it.
It tests language, historical knowledge, loyalty,
then implodes. The fumes off the river.
A child playing on a hand-me-down bike.
A washing machine. Bright cheeks. Living.

Those breezes. We know where we are, don't I.
I, we, tasting our surroundings. Where we too . . .
first steps. Gone. Arms manufacturers,
the makers of computers and software.
And God too, with children.
The oldest mother who
hasn't seen this all. Behind
the walls of her home,
watching the finances.
hoping to make ends meet.
Veils of light if you like.
Withheld is not restrained.
And those who would need power
to answer their fall, their loss. The song of earth
long-gone for them. Call it back. Kill none.

We enjoy the sweet fruits
of dry, hot places. The palms
and aqueducts, the lighthouse minarets,
the reach into affirmation of God. Bright fruit
and bright birds and intricate patterns
that aren't wealth but being, the will of the heavens.
Those intricate weapons that fall
brutally down, rough with cruelty.
Artisan dystopia. The weapons factory
in Vermont, or the Urals, or among the vines
of France, or entwined in the rail or road network
of Britain, or the bomb-makers' arrogant hands
steady in a mudhut, gloating over the constraints,
deftness with limited 'tools'. Never heaven's shape.

The foundations will be the bodies
of children. Under new buildings. Rebuild.
Not even bones left to count. The lion
has retreated, and is eaten out of house
and home. The eternal royal hunt,
with courtiers coming from their
own disaffection, their own failure
of choice, their sons swinging
the sword they themselves
had used to hack their way
out of the womb. Forgive them.
Raise them to the light. Let them
fester and ripen and sweeten under the harsh light
of an overly familiar sun, let them warm with the rest of us,
leave no one behind. But most, such vast numbers of most,
are glorious and living with a knowledge
of harmony and hope and sharing and light
and we can never close them out. Us out.
You and I. We are here for us all. Then rest.

Examine Thyself, Singing Honeyeater Villanelle [a variation]

Examine thyself, singing honeyeater
attended and not harried by half-a-dozen
silvereyes flurrying excitedly about this loner.

Alone this singing honeyeater comes in over
the hills and paddocks, into geraniums, is all meditation—
examine thyself, singing honeyeater!

Alone this singing honeyeater is a singer
of a differing song with greater and lesser syllables drawn on—
silvereyes flurrying excitedly about this loner.

It was surely part of a flock or a pair,
it surely hasn't spent life since the nest alone from its 'own'—
examine thyself, singing honeyeater?

But what if it has—that is, been self-contained, a recluse, an outsider?
What if it prefers the company of silvereyes or other associations?
Silvereyes flurrying excitedly about this loner.

Large among the small birds weighing down the flower
and twig, feathers ruffled as singing an infinite canon—
examine thyself, singing honeyeater, and rejoice in silver-
eyes flurrying excitedly about your character.

Villanelle of the Little Black Cormorant Tree
for Tracy

Dozens of little black cormorants daylight roosting
on the dead-in-the-lake tree with its duckweed halo
the suburbs close around them with stilled ibises watching.

These cormorants are florets open and closed, some contemplating
difference as close friends dry their wings, the ß-keratins offering sap-flow—
dozens of little black cormorants daylight roosting.

Between the lakeshore and an islet, the cormorant tree is preparing
for mass ascension, that lift of surprise or agitation, a threat that rows
through suburbs close around it with stilled ibises watching.

So many encounters with humans who can't reach its branching
into the close air of all-breath, held together by slick diving birds of shared ego—
dozens of little black cormorants daylight roosting.

Its weight of numbers shows the faith of death's shaping—
the ringwork of growth that adds invisibly after the scherzo,
the suburbs close around them with stilled ibises watching.

White ibises fall to haunches to study behaviour of the tree in its weirding
way of life in death its offering of sanctuary, monopoly, expo!
Dozens of little black cormorants daylight roosting
as suburbs close around them with stilled ibises watching.

Against White Supremacists Co-opting Dylan Thomas's 'Do not go gentle into that good night'

Lines taken out of context can make darkness burn
For those who want to burn the world, but darkness
Is their slow burn, white lies their eruption.

And when leaflets fostering discrimination
Appear outside a wheatbelt supermarket, they gloss
Lines taken out of context and make a darkness burn.

But what most disturbs is that such leaflets remain
Or are browsed as the town broods under a glaze of tolerance—
Is it a slow burn before white lies trigger an eruption?

We share breath and relish the health to rise each day in turn,
Each day shared in sameness and difference,
But lines taken out of context can make darkness burn.

Every word of intolerance sold as 'warning' is the crimson
Shade of the day-to-day accretion of a rage that is not the rage for existence—
A slow burn, white lies their corruption.

Let words of life that urge a life continue to be a lexicon
Of day and night, light and dark, of overlaps in time's ingress—
Lines taken out of context can make darkness burn,
A slow burn, white lies their corruption.

Eclogue of Moon Before the Storm

for Tim

The moon is dark adapted
as red clouds herald late,
    a single flyer's single wing
buffeted and torn and tossed
    down to form a skin
between ink and record,
the sum of what's reflected.

Our search is dark adapted
where fire had edged the world,
    a rush of darkening gale
leaving no time for adjustment.
    Un-nocturnal birds fly away,
lopsided into scrawl—a venation

    of collapsed sky-writing,
    a gall of vaticination.

The Sheep of ∞

On the east side of the hill rising
above the east bank of the brook,
sheep have carved an infinity
laid down as a conclusive '8'.

We recognise many of the same
sheep, though some have been
taken away, and others have grown
from lambs to what some see

as anomalous adulthood. There
is no humanly discernible reason
for this signing, the carving
of a pattern that goes nowhere.

But these are the sheep of infinity,
where the infinite is the collapsing
of numbered days into the endless
walk—branding earthly limits.

Off. Near.

'Screech Owl' (Eastern Barn Owl) During Ingmar Bergman's *The Magician*

Nothing magic about it, but I stop the movie
to listen because the long-out-of-date tech

the movie the machine the moving art is nothing
on the late night interruption of the screech

owl positioning itself outside the house likely
in the York gum just south of the Great Tank

preparing to drop down tiers of valley wall
through gnarls of shadow the moon past prime.

It's an interruption that opens hope for all works
and nights of valley ways, the small community

of disassociation and its edgy living, its distress
of semi-older ways and those new that are comforts

in being away from a centre of things where
nothing thrives anyway but here the *screech*

and then *screech* repeated is the warning
and summoning we want to take to heart,

its mesmerist's eyes uncloaking night
to show what forces don't have to be

harnessed as 'powers' but are there in their
own rights and not ours to own any more

than their own splice of surprise and apprehension,
and wonder and rodent fear, a most bizarre

mix of compulsion and tendency,
of dark matter and body heat.

Thinking Over the Missing Sixth Eclogue of Miklós Radnóti

'I lived on this earth in an age
when the poet too just kept his silence
and wailed, maybe to find his voice again—'
    —from 'Fragment' (May 19, 1944, translated by Emery George)

There are many poets voicing
out of isolation or demi-isolation
or ranging around and about isolation: all types.
How silent we are together in our lonely speech,
our shouting into disrupted winds, the range of spread.

Speaking out will likely bring consequence
when services are resumed as close to *normal*
as possible—an untenable normalcy we'll slip back into
by degrees unless in a 'migrant camp', war zone, place empty of food;
the configuration of want and lack and voice and who takes it out to be heard
                              by the *outside world.*

Outside world outside earth the orbiting electric car
the gall of litigation to bully into shape a 'free world'. Launch!
Which is more terrible, our words or the prophets', the silence
more articulate than our rousing parcels of speech, our gifts of eye and ear, sense?
The rain speaks loudly but burns, or drifts like salivation to make its mark—

Trying to write outside so the dates of composition do service,
bear the burden of interpretation you want to have but escape, elevating—
what benefits to survival the outliers of humanity post- you or me?
Dynasty-makers wish to ensure legacies yield like war bonds.
This age of world I inhabit leaves us garbling at the edges.

Exoskeletons

Words are less inherently
appealing less appealing
inherently only as skin
needing to graft extra
senses though likely that's
too harsh an abrasive rub
of wild oats and seed spikes

through socks wandering
the routes of machine
to home-usage, chains
of command that take and give
but mainly take, all falling
before the trimmer cable
flayed out of speech;

The whole frame shudders
and vibrates though
fingers don't ease the ache
of hinges, to work
with or against the gradient
is semantics
for micro-climates;

A metal eyelet lost on
a hillside enacts self-
protection to deport
as raw material and not object
as commodity one step
closer to origins & answer.
I search futility.

Walking a steep incline
friendship is never closer
or further than slipping
back into one's own foot-
marks; holds let go

one by one as subject-tracing
a journey that can't begin.

All of the seed falling
and so much needed &
unwanted, the scattering
of figuratives to make
greenhouses of silos
rather than places of
storage, contra-excursives.

It's like that turning
of year at higher revolutions,
that fling of covers—
similes were invented as
a way in or way out, a relief
or substitute from labour.
Cuts, callouses, a trapdoor

spider pulling back down
as I approach, but I—
you—we—will go 'round
its circuit, its ambit
and orbit, its influence
where crossing-over is
to be stung and dragged down,

dissolved and supped on.
Exoskeletons—invertebrate
refrain till the interior
pushed back into light
collapses and compresses,
which is the powerhouse
of geo and orbit

via a state of health
to reclaim body or soul

and yet let go of that claim
on first-aid or medicaments,
exercising rights of
passage and abode as
substitutes for conscience.

Writing for Insects

Trapped in my liberty
of reading insect script,
wanting to go through the eye
of the funnel into a network
of tunnels, spontaneous
to altered metrics
as if *fait accompli*
is acceptance, an aural
remedy to descent after
a global mockery
of higher things of the air (fowl),
brought down or sucked
into turbines; you might say,
I'm writing for creatures
that won't read me in their
crevices or from under bark,
on rockfaces, in burrows,
that they simply *can't*—but what
do you say to my placing
scrawled sheets of paper out
under the taut skies for breakdown
for mulching eating using for nests?
Isn't this a kind of reading
outside questions, those loose
grains of pollen that randomly
find no 'purpose' other than to meld
or affix, become an aside so pivotal
in this supervivid causality vs.
purposelessness.
I retract into singularity
every time I look for insect-sleep—
stark awake in the chrysalis,
changing rapidly and barely
changing at all from any
essential nature—winged
as sleep, but awake until exhausted
with writing, reading excretions, galleries,

pheromone trails, sheddings, those fractionations;
so many different languages
to write if not speak, adored;
and fewer and fewer insects
without birth or sleep, or
deceased with a warmth
moving ahead of itself.

Supervivid Header Fire Sestina

Another header fire—two thousand hectares
burnt out and the header a twisted charred wreck
which has the fighters talking of war zones
and a Vietnam vet, old now with cropping,
with sowing and spraying herbicides on the delusions
and evasions of broadacres, saying, 'Brought down by friendly fire.'

It sounds offensive and callous but history's fires
mingle with the smoke of a brash wheatcrop—hectares
of economic and critical theory, of wish-fulfilment, delusions
of grandeur, grains of truth. Later, examining the wreck,
a dry-mouthed and smoky neighbour insists that cropping
is doomed if chaff and dust isn't removed from the sensitive zones.

But the driver who managed to escape and occupies a zone
of embarrassment and anger, says, I blame the bearings—this fire
is the overheating of work is the risk we all run cropping
in the dry when dryness is essential to success—and these hectares
would have been downpayment on a new machine, this wreck's
insurance a self-damnation, a chuck in the towel, end of delusion.

Maintenance is mentioned. And not mentioning collateral damage is delusion
that will only stay in abeyance at the time of crisis—the fire zone
enveloped the crops of two neighbours, and their hopes have been wrecked.
And others who came from all over, all hands available to fight the fire,
crossed into heat and took risks, who arrived with water trucks across ashen
    hectares,
putting thoughts of blame to the back of their minds, needs must to save crops.

Birds scattering, and reptiles burnt on the treelines of crops,
insects on the firebreaks, sparks, the bits of life not wiped out—delusions
in the face of agriculture, the residence of unprofitable life a blight on hectares
of productivity, of manufactured 'fertility'—lost in the zone
of conflagration, and some mammals even shot on the edges of fire
and then there's the skeletal remains the animal analogy of the wreck.

An assessor might later say that it's strange that grass—a cereal—can wreck
a machine of metal and synthetics, and that late afternoon sun on a crop
due for harvest is a spark of beauty and bareness, an immanence of fire
and a hope to make a killing on a distant market, a delusion
of worldliness when the local is reshaped to make it a zone
of global agriculture with the topography of 'prior' written into the hectares.

Each year we hear of a header fire, and each year we see a photo of a wreck,
and each year the ash and char of burnt hectares and reports of lost cropping,
and each year the delusion that next season will bring a fire-free zone.

The Darkest Pastoral

I am walking concrete
channels through a city
I don't know pushing
through thinner and
thinner lighting till
I reach the semi-rural
edge then insect light
or slight reach of low-
wattage bulbs through
splits in air-raid 'black-
out' windows and stars
that have to work hard
far back to be bright
enough to show any
kind of way, then I am
stranded in an open area
that's still enclosure
and in an instant all-
consuming darkness
denies access to any
senses—just darkness
of the field darkness
of the pastoral and
the city (never a refuge)
a goading I wouldn't
even call 'memory',
that over-used and
inaccurate term
for the loss of time,
acts of recall—
the loss of habitat.

Listening to Hildegard von Bingen's 'O pastor animarum' and Thinking Over Dante's *Paradiso 23*: abseleration of presence

for Susan Stewart

As short as the absition of a shepherd's song
to pleasant and disturbed beginnings, mature silvereyes
voice the velocity and jounce of all wrongs

but for them this year has meant success
out of a nest in the geraniums—a pair of fledglings
that are flitting their demesne, to displace

and belong their paradox of light mixing
all holies and unholies, and what we see
in passing is the depth of a small flock annexing

and yet *letting go*, merging and quickly
reopening space, mutable vis-à-vis immutable
beyond analogies and analogues, our excuses; or, fly-

by-night utterances to heavenly bodies that crawl
across the sky as we fix ourselves in patterns—
no, it doesn't have to be this way, and to trail

after sources of light we don't need to determine
as separate, but as part of the same light we have
every time we imagine. So, I dreamt Beatrice said to Susan,

'Here is light, and it's the light of all suns' archives
across all night skies, and all light of reflection and all light
created inside our skin and sent beyond the *give*

of space, beyond its point of collapse. The fright
of realising that we should not have any right to escape
the trashing of the planet, the injustices we mete

out on each other, is more overwhelming than neap-
tide eyes of God.' And, so, I make poems for the protesters
in India who hand roses to the police who would tramp

down bodies and spirits—the joy of a flower,
just as on this trammelled place with its terrible
often denied history loud in the ears of sufferers,

we discover a flower that's not opened its petals
to us before, and though it is 'alien', it has been resident
since the nineteenth century and 'belongs' as little

and as much as we do, that paradox that is not, a false
anomaly in the 'settler' desire for resolution
the settler cannot have—but that flower is a gentle

if stunning blue—Cape bluebell blue—with all contradiction
woven inside itself, meagre against thin soil over granite,
an out of synch 'Regina coeli' equivalent with no answer; but protestations

worked through and addressed might make the song lift as light
at the increase of wrong times of year, and in the poem
we anatomise and at least announce that we care, that we respect
we appreciate we acknowledge, that we are grateful and will not presume.

Psalms of Sleep: a psalmistry

PSALM 4. TO THE LEAD MUSICIAN OF NEGINOTH. SELAH.

Hear me plead righteousness, God;
as I increase I grow out of distress via you,
hear me singing this prayer.

All twists from truth when we lose good
to shame, and I can but ask all that is endless
against pursuit of vanity and profit, quietly doing our own thing? Selah.

And knowing the Lord has set aside a place
for those who are godly brings me hope of recanting this unowned space.
To hear the silence singing.

Out of my sleeplessness, I yearn for the world unfolding
without intervention of greed, and converse with this hope,
curled into a question without doubt as my distress rests in you. Selah.

To claim no special treatment in your less impacting ways
which are not less than many others—trust in grace to lighten the tread.

And when despair overtakes and the desire for more and more
sweeps in to offset a perception of lack, fill the lost's faces
with the warmth of your face that won't burn.

For all the temporary abundance of a reconfigured planet
the bright produce on trestles fades before your bounty.

And shedding anxiety and flames that light the darkness
of the room I close myself into searching for emptiness, I will
let go and embrace sleep in safety of renewal and hope, O Lord.

PSALM 13. TO THE LEAD MUSICIAN.

Will all time pass before you remember me, before you reveal
your face again, O Lord?

How long will the loss of the world around me fill my soul
make a forest of thoughts where there is no forest outside me?
How many days will pass while enemies of life offer life on a plate?

I need you to reach into the emptiness I feel with disaster
with collapse I need you to fill it with light that grows outside,
I need to be free of the death-in-life sleep.

Otherwise, the exploiters will say they bought my vote,
the profiteers will say I have validated their product.

But I know the wrongs of wealth and property will be seen
on the verge of calamity and I will rejoice with others in your generosity.

I will sing long and loud silently and outwardly
because there is still air to breathe and water to drink, O Lord.

PSALM 121. A SONG OF STEPS

When the valley is under stress from gun and chainsaw
I look to the hilltops for a resetting of sunset.

Help comes to this location from all locations all over,
flowing in from the heavens over the earth.

But your foothold will never slip into the wastes
of the rapacious for matter is yours and never sleeps.

God of all the world of all peoples never slumbers
or sleeps and the message of a shared fate echoes.

There is sanctuary in the shade from the side
of house tree rock hills down through the valley.

And there's time to slow and stop the burden of destruction
we have imposed on the sun and the moon—to *live*.

For the evil comes in so easily so readily via the consuming
of illustrations to decorate our living—our souls aren't in those objects.

Step up to praise the sun but don't mimic it, step down
to let others climb the same steps without manufacturing more—O Lord, forever.

PSALM 127. A SONG OF STEPS

The house won't stand without foundations of trust
and the town won't work if people guard only their own.

The insomnia that wracks your life is a strange greed of wakefulness
so difficult to shake in the lateness where body eats dark & light alike.

And children are the gift that is the tree of life, O Lord,
growing through wakefulness and sleep alike.

In laying down their weapons the once powerful become more powerful
in claiming no more than the rights of their own consciences, in not *owning*
    their offspring.

For the children are peacefully and strongly marching against the violence
and rapacity of those who rule over them, and they ask for a chance to be heard.

as interpreted and versioned by John Kinsella

Indexing

Indexing *The Land Selector's Guide to the Crown Lands*
of Western Australia . . . 'issued by direction of . . . Commissioner
of Crown Lands' in Perth By Authority of the Government Printer
1897. . . you might realise absence and sameness, that real estate
advertising, marketing, and government approvals
to 'develop' are much the same . . . that being colonial
has many degrees as well as many avenues of denial.

A garden, a dwelling, the particular aims, hopes, desires . . .
needs of the selector—orchards, root crops, transport infrastructure,
soil quality, size of . . . extent, locality . . . are variables of productivity
for building economic communities with all their threads
and subtexts, paratexts and separate indexes to separate
volumes. Resources. Sections. Extent. Agricultural districts.
Proximity to *The* Capital. Gazetting. Before and after surveys.

Approx. cost of clearing an acre of *such bush*. Well-watered
not so well-watered. Rainfall intensity. Lack. Compensated
by. Conditions. Worked. Blocks. Experimental Farms. Methods
improved, methods cropped. 'Mixed farming'. Opened for. Select:
cereals. It has been found. Has. Been. Found. 'by experience
that the cost of clearing lands timbered by salmon gums,
morrell, and gimlet wood is considerably reduced, owing

to the inflammable nature of those timbers.' Nature. Of. Those.
Timbers. See page. See megafires. Index error out on a limb. Future.
See: no woodlands not heavily timbered but crops and houses
and . . . atmosphere flammable. Chain reaction. Cascade. Ghost
in the Hellbox. Cravers of holdings. Conditional. Balance
to be paid. Down. Getting their own clause in. Theirs?
Ours? Improvements to rip & tear, grub & burn. Maximum

persons per acreage. No person under eighteen
to purchase. Lend lease war talk later—building up
to quota, supply, drafts. Forfeits. Rentals and even freebies
as in Mt Bruce when on the bare bones had us consider
at least. Us. Them. Now payable. Within expiry
date. Or waived through landscaping
        the index.

Eclogue of the 'Big Garden'

for Alan

FARM

The big rigs the big plants the big bins the big yields—
across the stubble-sharp ground the duel duels churlish
but blunt as ambition, no time for hesitation, dragging
the seeder the wishes and predictions, the first-rains-hope
running out as we seed dry daring rain to come
as from eucalyptus fringes the ringneck parrots call.
What you hear is the diesel caul and the delivery of smoko.

CITY

The school takes us in with open arms with spread wings
if the fees keep rolling in rolling like the header across
the grand design the prayer plan for grain accumulation—behave!—
full silos!—for a low 'foreign matter' count at testing time.
As removed as holidays, the thinking back the envisaging
life as it departs from the furrows from the turn of the tractor
ǝʌɐɥ llᴉʍ sʞɔoppɐd ʇsǝʞuɐlq ʇsǝᵷɹɐl ǝɥʇ uǝʌǝ ɥɔᴉɥʍ sɹǝuɹoɔ ɟo ʎʇᴉuᴉɟuᴉ ǝɥʇ

FARM

We could do with the extra hands we could do with the kids
being at home but we do this to give them another path out of windrows
and burning-off the big garden that we love and can't see our
way out of the chaff, all contradictions we have foisted in front of us
the spray drum anathemas the conservative politics because
we can't see how else but be conservative, the kids down
in the city hundreds of ks away are going to stray, we know
but warn them against that road taken though we know, we know.

CITY

Rather be reading Judith Wright than fencing
rather be reading Jack Davis than herding
rather find my own way through though a few
extra dollars from hours spent out there is a sunset
in my pocket is the oily residue of ad hoc repairs
is the hessian windbreak over thin bare topsoil
is the glint off the shed when the galahs make an eclipse.
Taste the superphosphate, smell the chook pen,
fret over the fruit trees, tap the water tanks . . .

FARM

Each compulsion to control to eradicate
is legacy is leeway is prestige is kudos
down there with the city kids, we know,
and who is to call them out when we
did it ourselves as young ones—the stamping
out of the mouse plagues, the trophyism
that seems like warning and a forgotten
bill of isolation, a speaking out from space?
They think they grow out of it and we are stuck
on the back of the ute with a spotlight,
but we do it for them, we do *we* do. We see,
we see the wrong and the right of it. We make
the call, and set the alarm earlier and earlier.
They grow away from our ways though we
want the oldest one to come back to us,
to come back and take on the strain,
to say, This is my calling, I am expected.
The voice they expect us to use up here,
but we don't, we are caught in conventions
in the pastoral just as they wish it away.

CITY

I am *not* going back—only to visit
for special occasions, to show off my
lover, my new pact and love that isn't
a farm broken up across title deeds,
with erosions and salinity that are damned
if you do damned if you don't, trenched
to drain the dry when the downpour
comes and makes lowland a quagmire.
I have suggestions—stuff I have learned . . .
trees to plant, more precision, the place
of community art, a revolution
in the sports centre, so far away.
But no, I will go elsewhere
and *remember*, recall where
I came from, its immensity,
its imprint, its impression
of industry in the big garden
so far from the city, from small towns.
This artifice we are dragged into.

Eclogue of the Garden Phoenix

'From this session interdict
Every fowl of tyrant wing,
Save the eagle, feather'd king;
Keep the obsequy so strict.'
—William Shakespeare

That mood can so inflect the garden
inflects, drags you into the prisms.
of the house, and even the garden
verandah light on, and a massive
and shook leaves with feathers
I know it was a barn owl for though
of night around here moves like that
don't hunt that way. I disturbed
'The Phoenix and the Turtle'
make you hesitate before stepping
In guilt of presence shades stir.
caught around the window lit
pellets after the morning watering,
would never mock the garden,
taste, unless they get desperate,
I tell them that these seeds are true
they are vulnerable to the exposure
the hybrid ploy of disease resistance,
But 'true to parents' and 'true to type'
and dragged out of the enclosure,
Garden is where soul is tested
recover from' accruals disperse
the exception that you fear will
in a rush to get to end's new beginning.
with anguish and second-guessing.
as affection for any growth confuses
for itself, not its origins. But I obsess
and degrees of mutability. And I fear
philosophies that arise from analogies.
or flower no matter what, I will find
policies, the defiance of husbandry.
given laid out waiting to be spoiled,

as precious water on precious leaves
Last night, a tread in the air and a beating
trembled. I went out into the dark,
barn owl spread shadow wings
and arced down into the valley.
its face was hidden from me, no bird
and eagles don't fly at night,
myself with lines from Shakespeare's
because unfamiliar night sounds
into darkness. Isolation swerves.
Atlas moths—not their naming—
by a movie. I search for owl
and bronzewings tell me they
that the seed I plant is not to their
adding the wise caveat that they might.
to themselves and true to us, too—
of here out of place, and don't carry
of better and stronger and dead-ended.
are verbal tools of gardening realities,
we need to be wary how they grow.
garden is where the 'I will never
with pollen from a bolting exception,
become the norm, the whole crop
That's open pollinated overwritten
No F1 hybrids to distract your cause
pictures of purity—love the creation
over prehistory and cause and effect
the abuses of genetics, the social
I will love the reaching root, leaf
relief in growth escaped from containment
The stale historicising of gardens
the nuclear flowers aching underground,

the mushroom cloud we archive
version of creation or apocalypse,
a graphing of imagination's limits,
stretching and curving and planting
year's beans and peas were and moving
getting a long-term grip, and glorious
that the only manures in my fallows
and drought, which fallows its lexicon.
a possible future, a pseudo-plenty
of subtexts and echoes. I cannot
myself why the dry-seeded paddocks
urgent beds of green upstarts? This
of the tractor driver, air-seeder throwing
evocation of fire in dust, the ash
around each specimen—votive,
that yield a compost pit at best,
accumulated across
agriculture—'a poor harvest'—

as frontispiece or plates for an illustrated
as if it's a loop, a doughnut, a pretzel,
disembarking from the point to point,
nitrogen-hungry plants where last
crops to avoid 'pests' (those nematodes!)
fallow of the strip system except
are bird and insect and reptile droppings
But I am looking ahead—gleaning
to emulate the sun in these plantings
find an owl pellet. I cannot ask
across the valley seem to stare at these
feeding thing this emotional starvation
up a dust storm, the stomach-churning
from last 'winter' I sprinkle
oracular, offerings to the self
or wither away into stats
a century of invasive
to live to die to live by?

Eclogue of Fire

'Sicelides Musae, paulo maiora canamus!'
   —Virgil, Eclogue 4

'A camp fire binds us
Swapping yarns'
   —Charmaine Papertalk Green (writing of her community, the Yamaji people)

SOUL

Out of kilter the fire of wildness,
the kindling of birth we celebrate
such as Villon's 'Épître' to the courtly
child, heavenly conception we announce
the fact in itself of all births, all children,
none elevated above the other and yet
the favours that accrue in government,
the smoke of burning off the wavering
lines in front of a sunny day as aftermath
and what's to come if we don't make epistles
of denial—the birthing rooms of irony,
the bringing to life in a world we burn,
a Golden Age of seventh lines to herald
the new leader who will declare yet
another way through and maintain
or super-increase profits. Humanity's
wiggle room under the sun, the misplaces
of history where we keep position
before falling to crimes of silence.
Learn from the oldest voices
of place passed down—the interface
of knowledge burnt is the hellraising
roused by the zeal of words, a word.
Our relationship to the Golden Age
which is the age of fire and suffocation
needs to be reconfigured, an undoing
of the grammar of proximity,
and the figurative realigned
so the sap can course through bodies.
Respect, not copyright. Fire, not conflagration.

SELF

When I was nine I watched fire burning
through 'relieving rain', which vaporised
as it does now shown on the radar before
it even hits the ground. And then older
relatives were gone out fighting with truck
and water tank and pump and shovel
and wet hessian sack. Through the crops
with anger, and don't think for a moment
the firefighters almost destroyed didn't
anthropomorphise, because they did.
Most didn't give a damn about the niceties
of rhetoric and device and its broader
implications to the world. World was burning,
which didn't make one firefighter's politics
any better than another's however affirming
or negating they might be in ordinary
conversation. In the extraordinary,
the puzzle shifts and positions collapse
into each other. Skin and hair and even bones
burn fast, and a loss is a loss as the caught
animals burn, nesting hollows burst and relapse
into the idea of a future generation. Since
then, I have seen many out of control fires—
bush fires. At twelve I hid under a blanket
in the back of a station wagon as fire burnt
either side of a country road. I have sat
here, inside, not in the garden I try
to make lush in the dry with cooler
nights now, I try to make green against
the colours of burning. I have sat as I now stand,
watching flames and smoke across the valley,
working out how long it will take to reach us,
unless the wind shifts, unless the wind

shifts fire back on itself. And there are great
charred rings of older fires—of two
and three decades ago, when someone's carelessness
sparked a hill fire that ran and ran,
till it made another layer of record here, too—
a record over the immense traces
these split house foundations
can't suppress. Fire in the loop,
which is where we live. Inside a fire storm.

SOUL

You will wake to a sun image with wavy lines
through it—smoke warning. In the 'off-season'—
though there's no such thing now—the time
of 'controlled burns' . . . preparation as thrown
into wartalk, the only way they know. The attack
on supply-lines on undergrowth on 'fuel load':
burning-off to save yourselves from the summers
of your making, these endless summers
of lovelessness. And on the smoke
will ride all the glittering gifts of *nature*—
the first word to deal with in any language—
those miniscule abreactions you might
call 'opportunistic'. But you've tapped
every other reservoir for 'resources', so
surely you're not surprised. No, I know
you're not. And they will ask you
the purpose of your research, what 'value
it has to the nation'. None. But to humanity?
You hope, you really hope, and your skin
burns with the shame of having to say so.

And I have seen the gorse burn out of control
across West Cork despite so many requests
even demands not to burn; and I've seen peat
fires smouldering over years that heat the core
of legitimacy to a record of allusions and museums.
And I have seen forest fires in central Ohio, and watch-
towers that shape themselves to inevitability,
and whole forests ghosts of consequence.
And I have seen pleasure boats burning
on the horizon and it hasn't been a romantic
interlude in speculative fiction loaded with warnings
we can't learn from because it is still entertainment.
And I have seen industrial fires and the eternal
flames of war, and I have seen and heard and smelt
and tasted and dreamt and relived the fires
that ate an entire town and district I lived in.
Fire is beyond the senses. It reaches us before
it is lit, before we perceive it, fuse it with sensibility.
And yet, fire is the writer of the body's obituary.

SOUL

When you saw the forest burning and the marri trees
exploding with the heat and a tiger snake feeling
towards you, you welcomed it with open arms
but it swept past, anger in its eyes at your
belief that danger made you want, and ceded
worlds within worlds to make them one.
It's not the fire, per se, but its prevalence,
its new absolutism, the boost of market
economics, of factory emissions, of your
rapid transport. I separate myself from you

and not even fire can anneal us—some things
will be burnt beyond recognition if you don't
pull back, the very laws that govern the spiritual
upset by your laws of rapacity, your jurisdictions
of greed. And now you sprinkle last year's
fire ash across the garden, hoping it will
decode the trace, open a path to greening.

SELF

We will stop the burning of what doesn't
need to be burnt to survive. We will enhance
the broader conversations over the nature of fire.
We will listen to each of us that knows ways
of fire nation-states have forced into forgetting.
We will know fire as propellant as literary device
of victory is false grammar. You will show
us how to love the air, to know the balance
of ash and dirt, of living tissue and sky.
We will merge abstraction with realism
and you shall not be forced into conflict.
Your golden age cannot be contained by us.
Vigour and sparkle and dynamism
will be a taxonomy of growth,
and fire a conceit for itself
or backdrop for billionaire-messianics.

SOUL

There are some fires we are not part of—
shouldn't be and can't be.
Fire contained in itself.
Fire as it speaks with people

who understand and respect it.
Fire that argues with those
who rouse it. Fire makes
and takes stories.
Fire *gardens*.

Not a God Only Ant Ode

Ants push god aside emerging from their many tunnels
in what we term a 'colony' while they don't—taking umbrage,
though having the grace to keep to their purpose, concomitant
with god emergent manifold and compelled across interlinked
tunnels with those mouths out of a constellation of gravel.

Over the hill, many different ant IDs cross lines of forage
and traces of godly pheromones paint the pictures many of us
externals don't see with our constrained sense of art. But we
pause to view the meat-ant carrying a moth carcass
eight times its weight and more again if comparing dimensions.

The smallest ants, with their long trails and separated
nests still keeping in contact, are not overwhelmed or squeezed
letting gods in or out, and communicate with more than antennae—
their whole being going into constant exchange. Rubbing. They are not
a machine, or parts of a machine, and are shamed by our definitions.

Odes breaking out of bare ground where ants are most intense sending
their spokes out, cutting through and wearing down through mass
repetition, are not god speaking through ants, but god speaking
as gods with ants, gathering information for use outside the pressing
matter of the collective. God doesn't favour the queen. All ants are godly.

Deterring ants from extending into *our* comfort zone, our dwelling,
is not a prayer-act, yet has characteristics of prayer as give and take. No
harm done, we want back our sense of having done the right thing,
the selfishness of worship. Blue butterfly passing over green-headed ant,
wasp hovering over bull ant—these are odes, but not the only odes.

Hölderlin Ghost Poem, Tübingen

I saw his ghost
In the tower

Because it had
Not been dark long

And plenty of people
Were looking around & about

For whatever; he curved
The square of window

And broke all restraints.
I lip-read his, I love you,

And felt lost to the crowd,
A small crowd and not

Quite full moon
Ladling a chilled Neckar.

It was all about fire
And treegods & night's

Long stretch. He would
Have kissed me

If I'd leant too far over,
Fallen and drowned.

I am sure he was sure
That he would have.

Clarity

To make it clear, I don't think there's anything mystical
about 'ghosts'—they are an isness. There's no secret code
or system of access, and they are there whether you want
them to be or not. They are enjambments within your narrative.

Take an act like walking up the gravel driveway, up the face
of the valley, a semi-zigzag. The incline means you enter
layers of atmosphere at a certain angle per pace and height.
It is atmospheric, you buffer with ghosts of magpies in that way.

What choice will I have but to hang around here when I am gone?
I am confident I will be sensitive to those passing through me
regarding how much of me they do or don't want contact with.
I might have to rise into the troposphere for sociopolitical

reasons, and out of ecological concern. I will try not to act
as glitter, but I naturally reflect solar heat back into space.
I have no agenda other than letting things grow without
my umbra, for *my* ghost not to block spirits whose place this is.

Photographing Ghosts

The photographs I don't take are full of them.
I used to take so many but didn't know till
after the fact. Oblivious. Now I won't risk it.
Everyone has their theories. Or maybe *awarenesses*.
As you'd expect, given what we put our bodies through.

I tell myself that leaves are shrivelling on lucerne
trees right where I'd be taking a photograph—
but this doesn't mean 'giving up the ghost'. I've
always found solace in clichés; they suggest
things will happen again or just keep on going.

Many mice are digging out front, judging
from the many holes that are appearing. I never
see them in action now. I could have maintained
the watch at twilight, hoping. And I am dysfunctional
at dawn and would see things that aren't there

or unable to make up their minds. Wanting
to know more but already knowing too much.
Strange how many seeds can be unearthed
from bare, baked ground. It's not an issue
of dormancy, but shape. Again, my arrogance.

Some are only husks brought to light—
you can see right through them, and so can I.
Flash photography is the ruse they see through.
Incredible how small they always are—a pixel. Or two.
The photographs I don't take are full of them.

Incognito

After the summer burn this rain so light
it evaporates before hitting the ground.
But summer isn't over and far across the continent
rain is falling so long and hard that ground
is immiscible with shapes that will never reform
in the same way. To travel incognito is to abbreviate
part of the self to meet conditions as you imagine
them, or as they might be. Subterfuge or safety?
At a time when travel is inhibited, your incognito
is like living as so many others are dying.

I can't speak of the places I've been when the sky
is turning shades of blue and grey, is fulminated red
or coping with breath of rockets in all their
deployments. How can a book end when there are
others being written, and in this fact you sign
your hope: a signature you've forgotten but scrolls
automatically. How glib is the Doppler radar?
The rituals I've resolved are those for preserving
the house—not against but out of calibration
with ants, mice and rabbits. The inner outer thing.

I diminish my vocabulary to expand my understanding
of these experiences of static and stillness.
A prognosis of native blue-banded bees which
have seemed absent from usual places this year.
A psychoanalysis of absence. A dereliction of cause,
a tribulation of effect. 'Doomscrolling' events into ellipses,
that state as opposed to graves that are memory.
How we hear the galloping disaster. How we tune in
and out. Our jump-cut vision. What we conceal and what
we know. No franchise, no spoils, but new notes for return flight.

Watching Dulac's *La Coquille et le Clergyman* and Thinking Over my Great-Grandmother Playing Piano to Accompany Silent Movies

I know this one wouldn't have reached the picture houses
of Perth, Western Australia, in 1928 or any years soon after.

Late in the wordless anyway. And the British Board of Film Censors
issuing its verdict: 'so cryptic as to be almost meaningless.

If there is a meaning, it is doubtless objectionable' might have
echoed in text out over the empire, as if the reels were flywheels,

its members keeping specimens in their kingdom, class and phylum.
In corsets. Even the Parisian surrealists shouting down

Germaine Dulac, calling her a cow! Harassers. Molesters.
Fantasists. Artaud with all his doubts still hanging out in the stalls,

hoping for serious applause, his screenplay on no billboards.
My great-grandmother interpreted as she played, or played

from a score in the flickering light. How would she have run
with this? Single mother, migrant, royalist, leftover Huguenot.

That lusty ethereal necromancer priest, the general stuffed
into his uniform, his wife as object pursued through the limits

of imagination, Genica Athanasiou's breasts exposed to collimated
gleam, shell scallop brassiere torn away, dangling in the clergyman's

murderous soft hands. Confession. Taking flight. Lost at sea.
Without time to censor, great-grandmother would have rolled

with the flow, piano keys matching the pace.

Synchronising *Eaux d'artifice* à la Kenneth Anger (1953)

As a small child I might have thought myself a water feature.
My mother was learning Italian and visited Mrs Bagliani
on Saturday mornings to improve fluency and accent.

I still haven't visited the Garden of the Villa d'Este in Tivoli.
At school I once pissed behind a wall because I was too
afraid to go into the toilets where I was 'royal flushed'

and called a 'poof' by a gang of *boys*. I had no interest
in costumes but relished painting hand-puppets.
I turned the very back of the back garden

into a set of dams, canals and aqueducts. I wasn't
to read Rousseau for many years. I lost a friend
to drowning and almost drowned myself

on a separate occasion. He drowned in the river
and I was pulled from the sea. The waterways
in the backyard were built in sand and couldn't

hold water for long so I had to keep the hose running.
Sun glinted off non-reflective surfaces and mirages
flowed like capital works. Fountains have never

evoked sexual imagery for me. They have meant relief
from engineering feats as acts of imperial prowess—
the water winning out, always. In the glare,

I often saw things in the abstract. Out on the water
I would grow disorientated staring at the shimmer.
There was always less water than it seemed in the taps

and hoses and we had to be wary of amoebic
meningitis. I could make rainbows and even when
I couldn't see their colours (being so dazzled) I sensed

the qualities of spectrum. I heard Vivaldi at around
eight in the morning, but could have heard Vivaldi earlier.
I watched black and white films set in Italy during

the eighteenth century, but can't remember where
or how. Gargoyles fascinated me and I never
thought of them as evil. I often ran away

but not from home. I helped the gardener
(on holidays and weekends) lay the metal pipes
to reticulate the school oval. It was bore water

and stained things readily. Grass was bronzed.
It's so dry out here as I near sixty years of age.
It's dry even during a 'wet year' when it's pissing down

on the tin roof—resoundingly, the gutters can't cope.
I have been reading historic fiction and listening
for ghosts. I am dazzled easily and write mono-
        chromatically, planning a new garden.

Emblem

The wreck in the valley
no longer has an emblem
but the script of the design
indicates an earlyish Ford.

Henry Ford was a racist,
an anti-Semite, whose eventual
'apology' was likely scripted
and signed by someone else.

The failure of an emblem
to stand for veracity—production-
line business, human
suffering as quotient.

To say Ford was a 'pacifist'
is like claiming the machine's
'neutrality' in the devastation
of country. And the absence

of an emblem doesn't change
origins of rancour. If
there's a shift in perception
it's only because insects

and field mice nest in the wreck,
vegetation sprouting through
its engine cavity. The loss
of the eponymous barely
            emblematic.

Tree Elegy Across the Biosphere in Memory of W.S. Merwin

Pollination against the seed to grow canopy
and mark place in shades of green—dry here to reflect
in glassine quartz chips in the off-red dirt where trees *tree*
as the forest is difference *there* green-inflected light you nurtured far
where volcanic would give name in poem or misty rain for each better-
suited frond of palm, its trunk, those particular roots. *Here*, so dry.

Not to have visited outside the lines you published,
strands of rain where trade winds dry as here easterlies
sap the energy of watering. It's where we read, as you knew,
where the single tree in a back garden opens out to all
trees momentarily safe, or at least alive, before the chop.
I knew a man who tried to make a suburban backyard into a palm house.

Arecaceae would seem like part of the joke as we measure
tank rungs and how many waterings left, aside from our drinking.
But you see them where farmhouses were built and lost or condemned
for varying reasons—twin date palms ('fate palms') thick and robust
and the scrabble of rubble and chimney between. But no habitat of like, just
    addendum.
Living in a shack there was a single great chestnut, not a walnut, out of place.

A chestnut introduced like a vision of walks, the tessellations
of light collected into prayer, which is where it began for you. And for others.
The mirror of any leaf, the flipside, the reverse, is the growing and falling
enigma—even here among the non-deciduous, dry leaves fall, stroke light.
Whole branches cut off from the supply when sap is difficult to supplement, create.
That vegetation cleared for plantation leaps shadows out of wasted soil, to scaffold.

Gardening. I have known so many gardeners who sought
to build hope out of the clearing, to remake an image of plenty,
of sharing fresh air and taking stale breath. Each quietly 'oracular', if in denial,
each afraid of drought though remembering greened light in their plans,
their reticulation, their watching the weather. To make a calm to spread—
there if we bother to look, to listen to the birds moving in and out, some staying.

You knew back gardens, and you knew the streets made bare, as they
are here—say, of Melbourne, green-gilled city, whose old planted trees become
    expendable?
Or where I am, huge chunks of bush grubbed out daily with excuses made
or not bothered with—hard to keep track of outside the shade of verandas, offices.
Or among the palms on another island, Réunion, the warning of offensive odour
though a beauty that might make an activist or remaker of demi-lost verse forms.

What is there in common, across the list of names, of species—growing
conditions, from a part of the world far from where they're coaxed into a differing
light? What is there in common if we're not in the place of writing,
and yet we are grown into, welded rhizome by rhizome? You cannot take
the first bird I see today—a yellow-rumped thornbill tuning in, foraging
for the rest of the small flock—any more than I would choose to. It tends the
    image.

Each cell an art to tempt and let be to rebuild the soil. But no profiling,
and no conflict. The straggly tenuous but tough contradictions of York gums'
outer reaches supple but brittle closer to a perception of where a heart might rest,
termites holding the strings of a pacemaker, split and opening out to tempt owlet
    nightjars—
I heard one calling from a broken limb at 10:49 the other night and you were still
    breathing,
sleeping your breath to the canopy of world? That near and far line of prayer.

Once, on a very small island, a coral island big enough for a dozen palms
and a colony of land crabs and two humans, the heart of a young palm
was torn out and handed over to the one unfamiliar with its form or taste.
He ate, and the palm was gone. Coconuts were spouting, finding and making
on the atoll, at the outer. Lugging vats of water up and down the valley wall,
I think this, and your line, a late line: 'nothing is missing'—a conclusion?

I wrote of that palmheart for a heart surgeon years ago because all elegies
are entwined, even those of different endocrines. The circulatory system of
    memorials.
If welcomed under the green light of plantings, the off-spectrum aspiration
against grief, I would have told you of the jam tree—*Acacia acuminata*—

because we are surrounded by them against the odds, and they come back,
thriving on disturbed ground, with trouble around them. Short-lived tree shrubs,

their rough bark exchanges codes of camouflage with stick insects, as I look
now and can't see beyond the idea of an insect being there, legs forward like
    antennae.
Rot here is powder rather than mulch, mostly. Saplings rise to spend time dying.
But some pull through and some will become part of the width of those great
    jarrahs
felled by ancestors, their essences pushing against climate to make good.
My 'you' can't be yours, but the moon and sun do their own syzygy for us all.

Language is vegetation. I knew a couple who screened their cedar kit home
from a country pub with a line then another line and another line of native trees.
I have a family who planted tens of thousands of trees to reclaim saltland
    settlement
hauled out of its deep sleeping, its subroots. I knew a person who filled empty
paddocks with trees deleted for a new suburb, next to the new suburb where
bushland had hung on against the trend, gone late. To have known morning in
    those places!

I know you'll have known this—how thick vegetation, the uprights and bends
of trees on a still morning, can enhance our ability to pick out the between notes
of birdwork. You wrote of clarity, and translated ornate forms, to be filled with a
    moment's
singularity. Respiration. Our greatest breath might be so low or a rasp like a storm
coming in to rejuvenate, to depart with cataclysm. And so we pass with varying
degrees of light, the need for oxygen in the dismantling of carbohydrates.

Night is eating of oxygen. But more, much more out in bare day. So in our sleep
we join the trees, wrapped in leaves and fronds, held out of consciousness by
    tendrils.
So we thank god for photosynthesis more than we thank god for the sun as itself?
Here, we have valley, we have curved rim of valley closing out, here we have a kite,
    too—
a black-shouldered kite that hovers above the infrequent powerlines and
    self-supply,

and here we have year building on year that is an aside to a past that builds in all
    directions.

The inner green of room cracked in the thermal economics of presence
that underwrites reflection in crops and their residues, a shattering of light
in glassy stubble, the march against concrete and lead, against ordnance
and conquest, just roots holding soil so dry it is tempted to lift as a plume
across the district, hungering after the great dust devil that took off a roof
and opened a house down near Picnic Hill Road not long after you passed.

Interior of wood of fallen branch of loosened fibres and machines striking out
from gravel shoulders to lay great flooded gums on creek beds a trickle of old
    seasons
green with algae, green with signatures of flow, the bridges where great roots
    held sway.
What remakes such wasted soil? We try local species and intertwine with olive trees.
And in our suppressed thoughts, palmistry is a lush future of shade and
    flycatchers
maintaining the relationship between mosquitoes and moisture. No toxins; no
    anti-growth.

Our night-lights out here stick out sharp—sore thumb exposure, a failure of
    perspective
of what is lured to the hot light. Mouth dry. We go away too and bring places
back in descriptions but we won't let them set root—they grow inside and reach
no light, this bright light that weakens accustoming eyes over time, straining
to pick out moss from lichen, which shields the granite boulders it breaks down.
Gradient cuts underfoot the echidna following termite galleries, interstices

of plumbed surface-sounds. We go back to the records, the old books, which are
    young
and would replace those earlier cuckoo sounds, the kickings-out in nests, the
    breaking
through of secret chambers—all here, too, like birth, but with an unanswered
    history,
or partially echoed and not fully addressed. This stuff we do with our souls to
    adjust

the fragments of bush to whose maps? To miss the kangaroo trail though it's
    before our eyes,
or the path of an elusive rain, or a lake whose existence you might request, hint
    at, question?

Diverse as the air after war is gone but we still can't breathe so something slips
or grafts. The stain. We rely on such conservancy, on gestures of repair and
    renewal
that regenerate, to sustain with hands-off learning to let be, to live alongside,
harvest no more than needs be. Such need manifests. Such sleep of passing
is the caveat, is the covenant is the testament of work that rains without a cloud
    in the sky.
Memorandum of walk of planting of tending: crowbar to break soil or soft cell,
    either way.

Mostly, people search for pathways to exemptions
so they can cut down protected trees. Mostly, people
search for ways to get around those thin laws so they
can bring down an old system of life. But here, too, we
want to keep the trees going against the trend of felling,
to give breath to those who stifle the art of growth.

Pollination with the grain to grow canopy
and mark place in shades of green—dry here to reflect
from fool's gold but grow gnarled out of off-red dirt we coax with seedlings
if rain sets green-inflected light you nurtured far from here, far where necessities
work outside the poem for each better-suited frond of palm frond, a eucalypt
    trunk,
any particular roots. Dry wet dry. Making growth to suit a soil's recovery.

Not the Postage Stamp of the Christmas Island Pipistrelle!

To drag you back into viability
mainland scientists descended
to haul you into a breeding colony.

But vanishing was fast, and the last
of your brethren we heard echo-locating
in August 2009. What on earth led

to your demise, so many now ask,
weltering through herbicides and pesticides,
closing their eyes as they drive past

pockets of vegetation being emptied
out, mined, harvested. World is your
island. World is a roost under

dried fronds of Arenga palms,
with your few-gram-body
the soft-spot of reminisce

and distress. What is vanity
in bringing one's self into the blank
mirror of clichés—

extinction shows nothing back,
nothing we can learn from,
nothing we can focus on,

make up, repair. This picture
in which you're edited out?
Who found you roosting

in that hollow of a *Syzygium*
nervosum. Why should they know
about the size of your testes, your voracity?

Night sleep. Day forage. In and out
of primary forest. So familiar,
and yet, the details, the reports,

then nothing. An ad in the personal
column of—to you in your space,
and to those people who lived

in and around you. Just passing through
from Cocos (Keeling) to the mainland,
but taken into custody by the Feds

at Christmas Island airport
because of a failure to cross back & forth
between material and spirit worlds.

No cultural lift, just loss of connect
on both planes. And yet, as your
echolocation reached across

the twilight before twilight
arrived, a waking sleep, moths
testing the walls of constraint,

I tuned in—haunting premonition
of loss, forage zone of the spiritually lost,
the vulnerable, the lonely. What family

will post your obituary—trapped
in descriptors and comparatives, analogies
and desperate metaphors? Your thin-

membraned wing, your other-materials nose,
your veined-ears, your fur—all brushed me
under interrogation as you pieced a life together

in your splendid isolation, a nation's
flexing of manifest destiny. Human refugees
floundering, lost in surrounding seas.

Red-capped Parrot Cynosure

Sunset in the valley
which is still sometime away

from 'official sunset',
this inland of an *earlier*

nautical twilight;
but at the fastigium

of the dead central limb
of a York gum

at the southwest corner
of the red shed

a red-capped parrot
highlights—or is highlighted

to my eye, but sure, not for me
specifically, its cynosure;

I've been hearing redcaps
but not seeing them lately,

their sound
so particular,

even alluring,
an affirmation

of being collectively
alive and present

for all complexities
of 'a sighting',

and yet, there it was, it is,
offsetting crisis,

boiling over
into the cooler

approach of night
as if as if as if.

Wild Sounds!

Splendid blue fairy-wrens are mating and the female is pursuing the male
who is fighting his reflection in car mirrors and house windows! They are wild
with passion and compulsion and whatever else we might dig out to counter
our own vicariousness, but there's no getting away from it and a volume
and vocal-range never experienced by us here before is burning out
capeweed flowers and inciting insects to spontaneously generate
and spontaneously combust without any time passing for here
are the answers to particle physics here is the surge against all threat
to outlast the blasts of toxins and clearing and human solipsisms in the dilating
of the psyche hoping to plunder heaven for all it's worth but what's worth is here
exploding in wild sounds and wild moves and roleplay is busted and blued atoms
shifted.

Ghazal Not Gazelle

When a saying goes 'runs like the wind' and it's referring to a ghazal
and not a gazelle as there are no gazelles here and only *this* ghazal

Or the south-easterlies remorseless and gusting extreme fire risk
described as 'usual for this time of year' when nothing is usual in a ghazal

I shore up the rock wall but have to be careful where I take rocks from
as the valley wall adheres through large and small rocks, not ghazals

As I am working early in the day before the heat is entirely devastating—
the wind is still running as fast as a gazelle and global imagery coerces the ghazal

The trees around the house are horizontal with gusts and gutters are refilling
with dead or dying leaves—an urge to complete a work is channelled into this
   ghazal

With its furious intent the wind sounds like it's guzzling the valley
but it passes through and up and over and vents, inciting the heat of the ghazal

Sacred Kingfisher Diplopia Ghazal

Sacred kingfisher strikes spectrum into window pane but we don't know
what's happened—it duplicates, and we see it *this* time

Sacred kingfisher perches on the verandah rail, tracking insects
which double-image against glass and it strikes its rival, its own time

From inside the half-light of house we are part of the reflection
but, standing back, not part of a transparency, slightly out of its time

Its time. Subject object, insect. But kingfisher detects us just before
being swooped by a djiti djiti, turning to face origins, beak agape

Subject-object, angles of flight. Insects high-lit against polarised glass
now transparent with shifted perspective, and other birds doubled in time:

rufous whistler's warning call, yellow-rumped thornbills hopping
sudden over low scaffolds of dry grass; morning of insects and kingfisher time.

Ghazal of Shoring Up the Verandah

Shoring up the bank in front of the verandah, the bank under the creeper
the verandah relies on with the house relying on the verandah

Shoring up because the mice have made a network of tunnels
and shifted sand and excavated rocks to make nests under the verandah

Shoring up after studying the excavations in sunlight and halflight
from noon into dusk where last light is halved by valley walls around the verandah

Shoring up with rocks and small boulders and clay-soil-scrapings with mafic
qualities of duplex soil, that gneissic breakdown, I reinforce the verandah

Shoring up, don't for a moment think you're in a benign politics because you're
    not
and I'm not either—respecting the mice and even the transfer of rocks to
    verandah

Shoring up is to some extent a ruse you don't have as much choice over as you'd
    like—
hot under the collar, sun rising faster than usual, landscaping a poetics of
    verandahs

Imitating Rural Imitation: after Robert Browning's 'Two in the Campagna'

I

This place we live is termed 'rural'
or 'country-side' by arrangement
with or *of* the planters of grains,
the breeders of animals for
slaughter, by conservative vote.

II

But we're entangled among stalks
of wild oats, amidst firebreaks,
trying to coax that native bush
back to have its say, to undo
the rural we are entrenched in.

III

I always think of you when I'm
troubled by my presence—the rocks
that affect me but can't know me,
the marks of weather in the soil,
a honeyeater's heritage.

IV

I spend so much time both outdoors
and in studying those insects
which 'no one' seems to be very
familiar with, or rather feel
lost because they can't pin a name.

V

In this niche, this valley backed by
vast plains now made bare by yellow
De Stijl modified canola
framed as *science meets edibles*;
trials to boost outcomes ghost those genes.

VI

And I don't forget each day as
it runs into night, as each leaf
floats or is tossed onto the roof,
as the possum rearranges
to suit its own intensities.

VII

Can it be said that we have known
ourselves beneath the ghostly trees,
a fertility in the dry
sclerophyll forest? With such mixed
experience, interlaced thoughts?

VIII

There is a politics to our
presence; there is repetition
in how we interpret that first
welcome and what was done in its
name by those who made the rural.

IX

I so easily enjoy food
you make, so readily 'partake'.
The interjections of labour.
The less than synchronous bodies
that we arrange in this setting.

X

Inexorably, but often
joyfully, said once then again—
that reassurance we locate
in greenness rising from that dirt—
tautology *and* paradox.

XI

The first lashes of a spider
flower, planted in specks of fool's
gold, a glitter that pierces cloud
to send sun back, overheating.
We are within that red assay.

XII

What did we learn in Rome that we
can't learn here? The ruins of farms,
the ruination of ideas
fusing 'agrarian' with 'song'?
That was already here.

Argonautica Inlandica

'Thence it spreads inland over a hilly country straight forward'
—[*The Argonautica*, Book II]

Inland is not necessarily
any more interior than coastal

plains, even beaches. But there
are interior beaches and they

are different. I am different
inside such a geography

and feel the sharp stones
under my feet, the waves

of exploration in my face.
These waves are seismic

and the digging up
is a utility of geology.

I never feel ennui,
I feel alarm. If there's

no therapeutic term
for this, it's not hard

to wonder why. As said:
follow the money trail.

My father knows the mines
but I have nothing to prove to him.

He long gave up expecting this—
we get on well now. He lives

on an estuary, I live inland
but not utterly inland.

The extravagant rectitude of bees

The extravagant rectitude of bees
in the hollow of a middle-aged York gum:

over the decade I have fallen
before them, stung, full of regret;

membranes of x-rays
rapid sketches of transit.

They've changed the way I see:
where they've been is always

before me. A different sense
of temperature doesn't alter

with eye-scan and aura,
with impression of avoidance—

azure of the sky and chlorophyll of canopy
reddened in the cramped darkness.

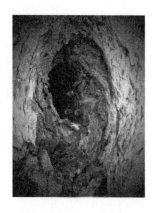

Torn abdomen, histamines.
I risk saying they are now

used to me. I slow wing
motion only to live longer

in resonant bands, blur
manna wattle pollen.

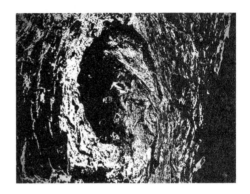

These patterns I word into fields,
smears lost in thumbprints;

autonomous as collectives,
glorious in memory of tree.

This portrait of descent,
realigning of exits.

Apotheoses and the Hölderlin Monument, Old Botanical Gardens, Tübingen

My father is in his last hours
and I stand beside the statue I don't want
      to pull down, have my photo
      taken. To *take* a photo. Or its past
participle. I am thinking of students
who almost worship the poet,
      and I am thinking of the missing
      arm of this 'Hellenic' Hölderlin,
which I learn held a laurel
before it was damaged, stolen.
      'Vandalised'. This happened
      in the nineteenth as well as
the twentieth century. All
that protrudes from the right
      shoulder is a tarnished metal pin.
      In Perth, my father has stopped
wanting to live. Last night he had another
stroke. He is in the private anguish
      of dying and wants it to remain private. Ergo,
      I wouldn't presume to talk about light,
and he wouldn't want to hear.
He never worshipped the old gods
      of Greece, and never wanted
      to climb Mount Parnassus.
He was the top apprentice
mechanic in Western Australia
      each year of his apprenticeship.
      He went to a minuscule bush school.
He lived with his mum, dad and sister
at Gleneagle where each was the other's
      lightning rod. Jarrah trees were monuments.
      He wouldn't have vandalised a statue
even if it made no sense to him.
Personally, I don't care what happens
      to a statue of an explorer
      or aristocrat, but I see the statue

of such a poet differently. I am
comfortable having my photo
        taken alongside it. But it's mounted
        in the old botanical gardens where trees
were sampled and cultivated from around
the world. The collectors have gone, many trees
        remain. The oldest tree is native
        to the region—a 250-year-old
beech tree. Its roots are uneasy.
It's not far from the God-like
        statue of or to Hölderlin, who suffered
        so much in his life and was no god.
He felt pain gods just can't feel.
My father's body is breaking down.
        And as he wants to leave life,
        it's not his will that's broken—
in fact, I am sure that it's thriving,
like the reach of the statue's
        missing limb, the laurel already
        bestowed upon us all,
whatever our failings,
whatever we've cherished.

Here Are Ambiguities

Here are the chaffinches we saw crossing the road dividing the forest.

Here are the blue-numbered logs we saw by the fast-flowing stream.

Here are the voles we saw moving through leaf litter, nibbling.

Here are red kites we heard high in the pines holding down their flight.

Here are fruit trees that sheltered us, shedding petals and forcing out new leaves.

Here are the plastic streamers that blocked our way, fluttering over the path.

Here are the gradations of those gauge boards as the water reached up.

Here are the meadows effusing and fermenting—spontaneously erupting.

Here is the mayfly on my hand bringing itself into synch with my biorhythms.

Here are the same steps redirected uphill taking so much more work—a test.

Here are horses being led by riders searching the forest for an inner light.

Here are resplendent blue beetles glowing next to a dead comrade—*to grieve?*

Here are blue stars evoking purple flags evoking white-winged flowers as aftermath.

Here is a record of passing as nettles vibrate and pine cones drop.

Rooks

Passing between brief clumps of pines
I am addled by complex discourse
       of the rookery —or two rookeries
       speaking within themselves
and also across each other.

With the sun consuming
the swan-form of Fastnet rock
       and lighthouse, the inlet
       brazen with sheen, it would
be too easy to frame as primarily
'occasional', a feuilleton

attached to the evergreen
while the serious hawthorn tree
       in the rocky right angle of a field
       speaks a politics of bareness
and the chthonic. *Note*
the rooks walking at the foot

of the hawthorn or filling every
spar of those pines. This is political,
       isn't it? Unique to a moment,
       making judgements,
stating positions, debating.

Graphology Heuristics 83: death by identification

Night parrots worked hard not to be found
by the invasive, the 'protective' and the exploitative.
'Found', they know for certain they are extinct.

ACKNOWLEDGEMENTS

Thanks to the editors of my poetry collections from which these poems have been selected—those collections range across forty-five years, a number of countries and many books. Special thanks to my long-term editor at Norton, Jill Bialosky, who saw my first US selected poems through to publication in 2004. Thanks to Arc Publications (UK), Salt Publishing, Vagabond Press, University of Queensland Press, University of Western Australia Press, Peepal Tree Press, and Picador. Thanks to my partner, Tracy Ryan. Thanks to Tim Kinsella for his diligent read-through. Sadly, Marjorie Perloff passed away while this volume was in press. To celebrate her memory and support for so many poets across the many decades, I dedicate this volume to her. Thanks to *The New Yorker* and the *Times Literary Supplement* for the uncollected poems included here ('Here are the Ambiguities' and 'Rooks'). Special thanks to Turtle Point Press for permission to publish 'Apotheoses and the Hölderlin Monument, Old Botanical Gardens, Tübingen'. Thanks to Magabala Books and Charmaine Papertalk Green. Thanks to Kwame Dawes. Thanks to Curtin University; the University of Western Australia; Churchill College, University of Cambridge; Tübingen University; and Kenyon College in Gambier, Ohio. I acknowledge the Ballardong, Yued and Whadjuk Noongar peoples on whose Boodjas I so often live and write. I also acknowledge the Yamaji people on whose Barna I went to school and so often visit. My work arises from the belief that human rights, environmental rights, and animal rights are all interconnected and dependent on one another. I deeply respect First Nations knowledges and country. No poem I write is separated from the colonial histories that have so damaged the planet and corroded rights and brought dispossession. If I write, say, of the island of Réunion, it is with an awareness of the violence of colonialism and its brutal history of slavery which still impacts the communities of that place to the present day.

INDEX OF TITLES AND FIRST LINES